Creating Effective Relationships
A Basic Guide to Relationship Awareness Theory

Steven R. Phillips, Ph.D.

PERSONAL
STRENGTHS
PUBLISHING

Library of Congress Cataloging in Publication Data

Phillips, Steven R.
    Creating Effective Relationships: A Basic Guide to Relationship Awareness Theory

    Bibliography:
    1. Psychology   2. Training & Development

Library of Congress Card Catalog Number 90-064345

ISBN 0-9628732-0-9

© Copyright PSP 1990, 1992, 1994, 1996. All rights reserved in the U.S.A., Canada & Overseas. No part of this publication may be reproduced, stored in a retrieval system or transmitted in any form or by any means, electronic, mechanical, photocopying, recording, or otherwise, without the prior written permission of the publisher.
Published by Personal Strengths Publishing, Inc. P.O. Box 2605 Carlsbad, CA 92018-2605
(800) 624-7347 • (619) 730-7310* • FAX (619) 730-7368* E-MAIL PSP4SDI@aol.com
New area code will be (760) starting March 1997.

1st printing April, 1991.
2nd printing October, 1992.
3rd printing March, 1994.
4th printing October 1996.

Cover Design by Kent Mitchell.
Printed in the United States of America.

In Memoriam
Elias H. Porter, Ph.D.
1914-1987

Table of Contents

Acknowledgements — i.
How To Use This Book — iii.
Preface — v.

Chapter 1: Understanding Behavior — 1
Chapter 2: Understanding Motivation — 11
Chapter 3: Understanding Weaknesses — 27
Chapter 4: Understanding Conflict — 35
Chapter 5: Understanding Borrowed and "Mask" Relating Styles — 57
Chapter 6: Understanding Others — 69
Chapter 7: Understanding Work — 89
Chapter 8: Using Relationship Awareness Theory — 105

Appendices:

    Appendix A: Relationship Awareness Theory — 111
        by Dr. Elias H. Porter
    Appendix B: On the Development of Relationship Awareness Theory: A Personal Note — 117
        by Dr. Elias H. Porter
    Appendix C: Behaviorally Speaking — 127
        by Dr. Elias H. Porter

Acknowledgements

This book is the work of many hands. In addition to the support and encouragement of Sara Maloney, William L. Wallace, and Carole Kramer without whom this project would never have been undertaken, I would like to acknowledge the following individuals for the contributions they have made in the various stages of planning, developing, reading, and revising this book.

Robert ANderson, Courtaulds Coatings; Arlene Gray Blix, California State University, Fullerton; Arthur I. Casabianca, Federal General Services Administration; Michael & Sylvia Gallon, Personal Strengths Publishing, (UK) Ltd.; Fred Haskett, Texas Methodist Hospital System; Susan T. Henderson, Ocean Psychological Services; Sue Heuertz, Panhandle Eastern Corporation; Charlene May, Charlene May Associates; Susan McCoy, Strength Finders, Inc.; Don Miller, Lone Star Gas; Doug Pearson, Pearson Consulting Associates; Gary and Sandra Robinson, Personal Strengths Publishing, Canada; Marcia Shaw, Intentional Management; Michael D. Sheean Associates; Barri Wilner Standish, University of Maryland; Robert H. Tomkinson, III, Tomkinson & Associates.

How to Use This Book

This book was designed for you to use.

It contains a number of exercises that require you to write your answers in the spaces provided. These occur throughout the text and are clearly identified. We have tried to anticipate the amount of space that will be required to complete each exercise, but it may occur that you will have more to say about a given exercise than can easily fit within the existing space. If this does happen, please use additional paper and complete the exercise to your satisfaction.

The wide margins also provide space in which you can jot down your notes and thoughts while working with the book. We do want to stress that this is a *work*book, designed to give you practical experience in studying the material as well as a good understanding of Relationship Awareness Theory.

The book was revised to correct type errors. The theory and text were not changed. If you encounter any difficulties while using this book we encourage you to write to Personal Strengths Publishing at P.O. Box 397, Pacific Palisades, CA 90272-0397, and let us know.

We invite and welcome any and all comments, suggestions, and criticism which you have to offer.

Diana Foltz, Editor

Preface

Interpersonal relations are complex. While our relationships with others may bring us great joy, they can also cause great pain. Our ability to manage our interpersonal relationships may well be *the* single most important challenge we face in creating a successful life for ourselves and for those around us. Consider the following three true stories.

> *Arthur was 54 years old, had been married for 30 years to a woman he obviously loved, but had spent most of those years with feelings alternating between irritability, impatience, profound puzzlement and deep affection.*
>
> *Arthur had met Joanna in college. She was, indeed, the woman for him. So why was he so impatient with her? Even after all these years together, having shared love and life experiences, he still felt frustration when seemingly simple decisions were difficult for Joanna to make independently; and once she made them, she frequently reviewed her decision and questioned the wisdom of it.*
>
> *Was she really less intelligent than he had thought? That question on Arthur's mind often made him feel disloyal and emotionally withdrawn from her. On the other hand, he saw her as cooperative, thoughtful, well-read and reliably considerate.*
>
> *Arthur felt a nagging guilt for his judgmental feelings and hidden thoughts about his wife. He wanted to understand and rid himself of his unacceptable responses.*

> *Marguerite had been with a major company for ten years and had been told by her physician that she was showing the classic signs of stress...Marguerite...had always enjoyed her job and felt pride in getting the promotions and pay raises that had put her in a respected managerial position.*
>
> *In spite of all the rewards involved, she would go home at night to her family feeling tense and fatigued. She seemed unable to find the warm and caring feelings she once shared so spontaneously with her family. Her husband told her that she had become increasingly difficult to live with, that he could not tolerate the change in her since her latest promotion and that she must come to terms with what was wrong...*

From the "Casebook of Dr. Chase" by Loriene Chase. *Westways* (April, 1987). Copyright 1987, Automobile Club of Southern California, reproduction by permission, courtesy of *Westways*.

> *Martin...had worked for years toward a position on his company's board of directors and had performed exceptionally well. Upon reaching his goal, he was delighted at first, basking in the privileges that accompanied his new position. Martin had made it. He had a company car, a new and plush office, power and authority.*
>
> *There was one enormous agitation that he had not anticipated. He had to work for and respond to a division chief who was so harsh and critical that Martin began to wish he had never reached his long-desired goal. Martin felt trapped and inept and more unhappy than he could remember. Here was a thoroughly competent, productive man feeling emotionally browbeaten by a superior who could, without fail, find a flaw in any report submitted to him, no matter how trivial the detail. Martin felt discouraged, rejected, invalidated.*

These stories are typical of the difficulties in which we often find ourselves with others. We often find ourselves in unsatisfactory, difficult relationships, whether it's with the people closest to us in life or simply people we must learn to live and work with. We must learn to manage our relationships more successfully.

No single model, no set of theories can say all there is to be said about interpersonal relationships. Yet Relationship Awareness Theory, as developed over the last thirty years by Dr. Elias Porter, says as much as any single theory can about why people behave the way they do and the consequences of that behavior in interpersonal relations. As we come to understand how to look *behind* human behavior for the motivation that *causes* that behavior, we take a major step toward understanding ourselves and each other.

> *Once Arthur learned that his primary motivation involved task accomplishment, but that his wife was motivated by a desire to remain flexible, be a good team player and, above all else, keep her options open, he then understood that each of them had different ways of feeling good about themselves and could then learn to value his wife's motivation and behavior instead of imposing his own values on her.*

> *Once Marguerite learned that she felt best about herself when she could help and nurture others, she began to understand how her recent "success" was providing her with fewer and fewer opportunities to be helpful and was, in fact, demanding a whole new set of assertive behaviors that she did not find satisfying. She was then in a position either to reconsider in a new light the costs of this "success," both to her personally and to her marriage, or to begin to look for more opportunities to be helpful in her new position.*

> *Once Martin came to understand that his division chief felt best about himself when he could analyze in great detail and with great precision the work of others, not to tear others down, but instead to produce work of the highest level of accuracy and excellence, he knew how and why to respond to that need.*

An understanding of Relationship Awareness Theory can be perhaps the single most important step any of us can take toward improving our relationships with others. The purpose of this book is to help make that possible.

A Personal Note

I first came into contact with Relationship Awareness Theory as a participant in an otherwise long-forgotten conference held at least fifteen years ago. That first contact was not particularly meaningful for me. Perhaps because the presenter really did not understand the power of his material, perhaps because I was not yet ready to hear Dr. Porter's message, my first response was to dismiss Relationship Awareness Theory as yet another superficial attempt to classify human behavior under some neat but essentially meaningless labels (in this case, of course, Red, Blue, and Green).

About two years later I myself was in need of some material for a workshop I was about to present and, for some reason, dug out that old copy of the **Strength Deployment Inventory**. For whatever reason (probably having to do with my readiness to listen to the message of Relationship Awareness Theory), I began to discover the value of this material.

I began to see that far from being a superficial classification of human behavior, Relationship Awareness Theory provides a remarkable series of insights into understanding human *motivation* and how motivation *translates* into behavior.

Since that time I have presented this material to thousands of people in hundreds of workshops and seminars on human relations. The richness of this material and its ability to lead to self-discovery and to an understanding of others continues to excite me.

During his lifetime, Dr. Porter never wrote the book many of us in this field would have liked him to have written. The need for a single, comprehensive statement about Relationship Awareness Theory is, I believe, self-evident. I have no illusions that this is the book Dr. Porter would have written. As he himself stated many times, Relationship Awareness Theory is not yet finished. Perhaps the definitive discussion will never be written.

To the best of my ability, however, and with the active cooperation and assistance of his wife, Dr. Sara Maloney, I do believe that this book can stand as a useful and helpful statement of Dr. Porter's work.

The purpose of this book, therefore, is not to provide the authoritative statement on Relationship Awareness Theory. It is instead to offer a framework for self-discovery, a vehicle through which you can increase your understanding of interpersonal relationships. I am deeply grateful to Dr. Maloney and to Carole Kramer at Personal Strengths Publishing, Inc., for their assistance in developing this book and for giving me the opportunity to present Relationship Awareness Theory to you.

About the Developer of Relationship Awareness Theory

Elias H. Porter received his Ph.D. degree in Psychology from Ohio State University in 1941. While pursuing doctoral studies, he was appointed as an Assistant in psychology and taught a variety of courses. His dissertation advisor was Carl Rogers, Ph.D. He was at the University of Chicago for seven years, where he served as a staff member of the Counseling Center under the direction of Carl Rogers. Here he combined teaching with clinical work and editing a publication devoted to non-directive counseling. It was here also that he began his research in the self-concept which led to his development of Relationship Awareness Theory in early 1970.

Dr. Porter held teaching posts at the University of Oregon, the

University of California at San Diego, and University of California at Los Angeles. He served as associate clinical professor in the Department of Psychiatry, School of Medicine, University of California, Los Angeles and maintained a private practice through the years.

Dr. Porter's industrial and organizational experience included the positions of Assistant Director of Human Factors Directorate at System Development Corporation and Senior System Scientist at Technomics, Inc. He contributed material to several books and numerous scientific journals and authored two books: *Introduction to Therapeutic Counseling,* Houghton Mifflin, 1950, and *Manpower Development,* Harper and Rowe, 1964. In 1971 he founded Personal Strengths Publishing, Inc., and served as President of that company until his death in December, 1987.

About the Author

Steven R. Phillips received his Ph.D. in English Literature from the University of Rochester in Rochester, New York in 1969, and has taught English at the University of Rochester, Rockford College in Rockford, Illinois, and Alfred University in Alfred, New York.

Dr. Phillips has co-authored four books on professional and organizational development, including *Solutions: A Guide to Better Problem Solving* published by University Associates in 1987. He is currently President of Solutions Management, a training and development firm in Corvallis, Oregon. His clients have included such organizations as Lockheed, Hewlett-Packard, NASA, Nike, AMOCO, Chevron, the U. S. Forest Service, the U. S. Bureau of Mines, and the U. S. Army Corps of Engineers.

A Word About Trademarks

Relationship Awareness™ and Job Interactions Inventory™ are trademarks of Personal Strengths Publishing™, Inc.: Strength Deployment Inventory® and Feedback Edition® are registered trademarks of Personal Strengths Publishing, Inc. For purposes of readability, the trademark symbols have not been included in the text of this book. Additional copies of the **Strength Deployment Inventory** and other questionnaires and inventories mentioned in this book may be obtained from Personal Strengths Publishing, Inc., P.O. Box 2605 Carlsbad, CA 92018-2605 telephone (619) 730-7310* or (800) 624-7347, FAX (619) 730-7368*.

* New area code will be (760) starting March 1997.

Chapter One

Understanding Behavior

Relationship Awareness Theory is built on a single, fundamental assumption: behavior must not be viewed as an end in itself, but as a vehicle that moves each of us toward a greater sense of self-worth. Every human being interacts with others in ways that are intended to help that person feel good about himself or herself as a person.

The purpose of this book is to help you explore the implications of this assumption in understanding yourself, in understanding others, and in understanding yourself as a person in relationship with other people.

As you read the following chapters and apply Relationship Awareness Theory to your own life, please keep in mind the following major points:

- Look at your own behavior and the behavior of others as a vehicle for satisfying an important want or motivation.

- Consistency in interpersonal relations is found in the wants or motives of the individual, wants or motives that lie *behind* behavior.

- Understand others' behavior in terms of *their* motivations rather than your own.

- One thing we all have in common is the need to feel good about ourselves as people.

Remember: Relationship Awareness Theory is *for* you, not *about* you. Ask yourself how these ideas apply to you and to the people you know. Once you begin to *apply* these ideas to your relationships, you can experience the power and value of Relationship Awareness Theory.

Chapter One

Four Basic Ideas

Relationship Awareness Theory is built upon four basic ideas.

First, and most importantly, we want to feel worthwhile about ourselves as people. Understanding interpersonal relationships involves understanding how we strive to find ways of interacting with each other that allow us to feel good about ourselves. Some of us strive for this sense of self-worth effectively, some ineffectively. But no matter how successful or unsuccessful that behavior may be, everyone wants to feel worthwhile about himself or herself as a person.

Second, there are two quite different conditions that affect your behavior. The first of these conditions exists when things are going well for you and you are free to pursue what you want in your interactions with others. The second condition exists when you are faced with conflict or opposition and are no longer able to get what you want from others.

Third, a personal weakness is no more than the overdoing of a personal strength. One of the most profound insights of Relationship Awareness Theory is that a weakness is best understood as an inappropriate use of a strength. You don't need to "get rid" of a weakness; you need to learn not to overdo a strength.

> This idea was originally developed by Erich Fromm in the third chapter of *Man for Himself* (Holt, Rinehart & Winston: New York, 1947).

Fourth, the more clearly a personality theory explains and validates your own experience, the more effectively you can use the theory for self-discovery and for making your relationships more productive.

The Strength Deployment Inventory

This book has been written for people who have completed the **Strength Deployment Inventory,** and from this point on I assume that you have in hand a copy of that questionnaire with your current scores. Please write down in the space provided at the top of the next page your scores from the first page of the inventory, that is, your scores from columns one, two and three.

> If you do not have in hand a completed copy of this questionnaire with your current scores, you may wish to write Personal Strengths Publishing, Inc., P. O. Box 397, Pacific Palisades, California 90272 or call them at (310) 454-5915 to obtain a copy. Although it would be possible to read this book and thus learn something about Relationship Awareness Theory without having taken the **Strength Deployment Inventory**, this book will only be *personally* useful to you if you are willing to apply your scores to these ideas. You may use the mail order card at the back of this book to place your order.

Column One	Column Two	Column Three

Page one of the **Strength Deployment Inventory** provided you with an opportunity to describe the ways you behave when things are going well for you under a variety of circumstances: at work and at home, as well as in various social situations in which you feel good about yourself. (See top of page 2 of the SDI.) This chapter focuses on those scores from page one. A discussion of your behavior in the face of conflict and opposition appears in Chapter Four.

FOUR BASIC MOTIVATIONAL ORIENTATIONS

ALTRUISTIC-NURTURING (BLUE)

Look at your scores in columns one, two and three. If your score in any one of those three columns is a 57 or higher, there can be little doubt that you give first priority to that particular orientation. If that score is in column one (Altruistic-Nurturing) you are primarily motivated by a desire to be nurturant and what makes you feel worthwhile about yourself as a person is when you have an opportunity to be of genuine help to others.

ASSERTIVE-DIRECTING (RED)

If your score of 57 or higher is in column two (Assertive-Directing), you are primarily motivated by a desire to be a leader and what makes you feel worthwhile about yourself is when you are having an opportunity to run the show and get things done.

ANALYTIC-AUTONOMIZING (GREEN)

If your score of 57 or higher is in column three (Analytic-Autonomizing), you are primarily motivated by a desire to be self-sufficient and self-directed and what makes you feel worthwhile about yourself as a person is when you are able to think things through for yourself and bring a sense of logical orderliness to whatever you are doing.

FLEXIBLE-COHERING (HUB)

If all of your scores are in the 22-44 range (Flexible-Cohering), your primary gratification comes from the opportunity to be flexible, to explore a variety of options and possibilities and, perhaps, in your success at promoting group cohesiveness. You feel best about yourself as a person when you can keep your options open, when you can get people to all pull together, when you can get others to commit themselves to a common cause, and when you have the opportunity to take whatever role is necessary to accomplish that sense of group cohesiveness.

The Blends

If you have two scores of 33 or higher and your third score is 21 or lower, you would probably tend to blend together the motivations identified by those two higher scores. People whose scores are high in two orientations report that they often experience tension within themselves when interacting with others. Sometimes they combine the strengths from each and at other times they feel a pull toward the higher score.

If your highest two scores are in columns one and two (Assertive-Nurturing), you receive your greatest gratification from helping assertively. You provide what you believe people need. Often you surprise people by fighting for the underdog.

If your highest scores are in columns two and three (Judicious-Competing), you find satisfaction in combining competition with analysis through the development of strategies that help you to win by using your head.

If your highest two scores are in columns one and three (Cautious-Supporting) you find satisfaction in being helpful until you determine you have done enough. You want people to be self-dependent and you help towards that goal. You also protect yourself from giving what feels like too much of yourself.

The implications of these scores for you and for your relationships with others is what this book is all about.

"There is Nothing so Practical as a Good Theory"

Attributed to Kurt Lewin, one of the founders of behavioral science.

"The practical nature of a good theory" nicely describes the approach to Relationship Awareness Theory taken in this book. A theory exists not for its own sake but to explain something. The purpose of Relationship Awareness Theory is to *help us under-*

stand and manage our day to day relations with people. This is intended to be a practical book.

You must understand the theory. In order to begin to see how Relationship Awareness Theory can increase your awareness of your own behavior and the behavior of others, you need to understand these ideas and the ways in which they differ from other approaches to understanding human relations. Once you understand the basic concepts you can begin to build on them in ways that are practical and rewarding for you.

Behavioral Approaches to Understanding Human Relations

Most current theories of human relations focus strictly on behavior, which means they work this way:

> First, a person's behavior is assessed and characteristic patterns are identified;

> Second, those characteristic patterns or styles of behavior are categorized and labeled; and,

> Third, the person's behavior in new situations is predicted on the assumption that the best predictor of future behavior is past behavior.

This rather simplistic view of the relationship between past and future behavior can be represented as follows:

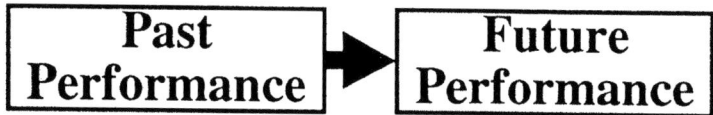

Such an approach to understanding human relations attempts to predict future behavior from consistencies in past behavior.

Of course, to the extent that the person's type is correctly identified, future behavior *can sometimes* be predicted, if not with 100% accuracy, then with at least enough accuracy to make it worthwhile to teach others that particular theory. One of Murphy's Laws states, "The race is not always to the swift nor the battle to the strong, but that's the way to bet." When all we have to go on is how a person has behaved in the past, the best bet for the future is to assume a continuation of that behavior.

This kind of thinking thus leads us into the habit of asking, "What would an 'extrovert' do in this situation?" or "How would an 'introvert' respond to that situation?" There are a number of problems with this kind of thinking.

First, such an approach leads to an oversimplification of human behavior. Human beings almost by definition transcend categories, and no label, no matter how ingenious, can describe the complexity of even a single human being. This is a reason why so many people resist most behavioral models. Although they will acknowledge that they often behave in ways described by a particular category, they also know that sometimes they do not behave in that way and thus appropriately reject the value of such an exercise.

> Perhaps the most glaring example of this kind of oversimplification involves labeling Blues, Reds and Greens as St. Bernards, Lions, and Owls. Such a use of this material trivializes the theory and reduces these concepts to little more than the level of a party game.

Second, any approach to human relations that limits itself strictly to behavior fails to take into account the fact that we are purposive beings. We strive for things. Most of us do go about trying to achieve our gratifications in characteristic and even predictable ways—as long as it serves our purposes to do so. But we may sometimes dramatically change the ways we act without ever changing our goals.

Third, a behavioral way of thinking does not answer the question "Why?" To say that an "extrovert" behaves in a certain way in a certain situation because he or she is an extrovert does not get us very far. What is needed is a theory or model of interpersonal relations that goes beyond behavior to motivation in order to answer the important question, "Why does a particular person behave in a particular way in a particular situation?"

Introducing Relationship Awareness Theory

In contrast, the approach Relationship Awareness Theory takes is quite different from those behavioral theories described above. Relationship Awareness Theory looks at behavior simply as the tools you use in order to get something you want or to avoid or escape something you don't want. The patterns of behavior that you develop in accomplishing these goals are then seen as more or less characteristic ways of responding to your current situation. Your behavior can change from time to time as needed to help you be more effective in getting what you want or avoiding what you don't want.

This relationship between behavior, values and the environment can be described visually as follows:

Predicting Future Performance

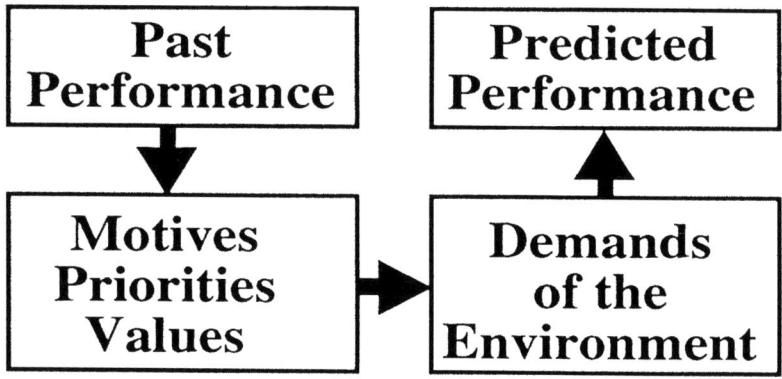

In other words, behavior can be best seen, not as an end in itself, but as the result of the interaction between what you value (your motives or priorities) and the rewards (or lack of rewards) available to you. If the environment provides plenty of opportunities to do things you value, you will probably do those things more frequently than you will do other things. But if those opportunities are not available, at least, not at the moment, you are free to change your behavior without changing your values.

People new to Relationship Awareness Theory often seem to use it as if it were nothing more than another way of describing behavior. Someone might say "Oh, he's a blue, so he'll offer to help," or "She's a red, so she will try to take charge," or "He's a green, so he'll stop to analyze it" or "She's a hub so she'll want to keep her options open." In each case the speaker has made the assumption that because someone is primarily motivated by a desire to be nurturant, or assertive, or analytical, or flexible, he or she will always and in every situation behave in a nurturant, assertive, analytical, or flexible way. The speaker has failed to understand that motivation lies behind behavior and that behavior may vary in pursuit of valued goals.

For purposes of readability, I will tend to refer in this book to the four primary orientations as Blue, Red, Green, and Hub rather than using such terms as "Altruistic-Nurturing." Please keep in mind, however, that these terms are used only as a shorthand way of referring to a complex set of behaviors and motives as described and explored throughout this book.

Just because someone is a Blue does not mean that he or she will always "offer to help." As a matter of fact, knowing that this individual is a Blue may be the basis for predicting that in a certain instance he or she would *not* offer help. To be sure,

This paragraph and the discussion that follows are based on a letter written by Dr. Porter to Michael C. Gallon, the director of Personal Strengths Publishing, England, and published in "The Training Officer," December, 1983.

Blues want their behavior to result in benefit to others, and they may accomplish this by "helping" behavior. They may also accomplish this, however, by saying "no" or by refusing to "help" if, in their judgment, that would be the best way to benefit the other person.

> *A caring, loving parent, to be helpful to her teen-age child, sets down and enforces with great strictness rules about appropriate dress and behavior.*

A Red person may in no way want to "be in charge" if there are no tasks to be accomplished, no resources to be managed, no authority given on which to act, or no responsibility assigned to achieve some goal. On the other hand, give a Red a serious task to accomplish, the authority to accomplish it, the resources he or she needs to get the task done, and you might well see that person bending over backwards to be directly helpful to someone who is a key person on the road to success. Reds want to get the job done whether they have to "lead, follow, or get the hell out of the way!"

> *A manager gently and patiently encourages a subordinate to learn a whole new technology so that the subordinate can accomplish an important part of the manager's project.*

A Green person is not going to waste time, energy or any other resource on putting into order that which is already in order. On the other hand, you might see a Green being very assertive in a relationship in support of a proven procedure.

> *An engineer becomes quite forceful and persuasive in getting others to see the logic of his solution to a difficult problem and becomes a champion throughout the entire corporation of the new product that results from that solution.*

And, finally, a Hub is not going to want to be flexible and keep his or her options open when the goal is certain and the path to reaching that goal is clearly laid out.

> *A civil servant, though valuing flexibility and teamwork, lays out a clear career plan which she pursues with focused determination.*

Behavior, then, is best seen not as an end in itself but as a vehicle that moves us toward feeling worthwhile about ourselves as human beings. For this reason, be very careful about describing someone only in terms of that individual's observed behavior. Constantly look behind that behavior for the motive or goal that is driving that behavior. Only in this way can we come to a fuller understanding of another person.

Conclusion

Relationship Awareness Theory can help you become more aware of what you are seeking (and seeking to avoid) in interpersonal relations. The more aware you can become of what you are striving for and the more aware you can become of what others are striving for, the more you can use your own strengths and the sometimes quite different strengths of others to achieve more productive interpersonal relationships.

In the next chapter we will take a closer look at Relationship Awareness Theory. In Chapter Three we will look at interpersonal conflict and at the meaning of your scores in columns four, five and six of the **Strength Deployment Inventory.** Subsequent chapters will then explore other aspects of Relationship Awareness Theory, always with an emphasis on the insight these ideas can provide you in understanding yourself and others.

Chapter Two

Understanding Motivation

In Chapter One you had an opportunity to begin exploring the meaning of your scores on the **Strength Deployment Inventory** when things were going well for you and you were feeling good about yourself as a person. You were then introduced to some of the ideas that lie behind Relationship Awareness Theory. This chapter now examines in greater detail the implications of these ideas for you and for your understanding of yourself as a person in relationship with others.

Every Person Is Like All Other Persons

One of the most important concepts in Relationship Awareness Theory is that every person is like all other persons in one important respect: all persons want to feel worthwhile about themselves as human beings. It is impossible to overemphasize that concept. If there is any one thing I would like you to learn from this book, it would be that each of us attempts to interact with others in our lives in ways that help us feel good about ourselves. This single idea is the key to understanding ourselves and each other, as well as to understanding Relationship Awareness Theory.

To demonstrate this important concept, I would like to get you involved in a brief activity. From time to time in this book, I will ask you to stop in your reading to reflect in a structured way on these ideas and on their meaning for you. In most cases you will be asked to write out some of those reflections and conclusions. *I strongly encourage you not to skip over these sections.* Relationship Awareness Theory is intended above all else to be practical and useful to you, to help you come to a better understanding of yourself in relationship to other people. *If you do not invest yourself in completing these activities, you miss much of what this book is about.*

For the first of these structured activities, then, I would like you to think for a few moments about people with whom you have worked or have socialized in the recent past. Now identify two or three people from work and two or three people from social situations with whom you feel good about yourself as a person, people who bring out the **best** in you. Write the names of those people in the spaces provided in the following table.

> Where appropriate, these activities have been reproduced and completed at the end of each chapter. The purpose of doing this is not in any way to suggest a "right" answer but instead to provide an example of how someone might go about completing that particular activity. Most of the time you will probably be able to go ahead with each activity on your own, but if you feel stuck and don't at first see a way to get going on that exercise, you may find these examples useful.

Chapter Two

People with whom I feel good about myself at work

1._____

2._____

3._____

People with whom I feel good about myself in social situations

1._____

2._____

3._____

In the space provided to the right of and below each name describe briefly what it is you do in these relationships that you enjoy and that promotes your feeling good about yourself as a person.
When you have finished, complete the following statement:

I most enjoy a relationship in which I can be

_____

_____

_____

_____

Finally, compare the statement you have just written with the brief description of the meaning of your scores at the beginning of the previous chapter. Do you see a clear and specific connection between what you describe as enjoyable for you in relationships and your scores on the **Strength Deployment Inventory**?

Every Person is Like Some Other Persons

Although each of us seeks to interact with others in ways that help us feel good about ourselves, not everyone feels good about himself or herself for the same reasons. In other words, what helps me feel good about myself as a person and what helps you feel good about yourself as a person may be quite different. Relationship Awareness Theory identifies four primary interpersonal orientations. Each orientation finds expression in what is called a *valued relating style,* a way of behaving that allows that individual to feel good about him or herself as a person.

Altruistic-Nurturing (Blue) Motivation. When an individual behaves in patterns of ways that can be characterized as trusting, optimistic, loyal, idealistic, helpful, modest, devoted, caring, supportive, accepting, and so on, that is, in ways that when taken together suggest that the individual places the enhancement of the welfare of others at the top of his or her priorities, we infer that his or her basic sense of self-worth comes from being nurturant of others without direct rewards in return.

> *A school teacher, upon retirement, looks back over the years and feels fulfilled through the number of children who "made it" because of what he was able to bring them. His primary concern was not for any personal reward other than clear evidence of having been of genuine help to those in need.*

Assertive-Directing (Red) Motivation. When an individual behaves in patterns of ways that can be characterized as self-confident, enterprising, ambitious, organizing, persuasive, forceful, quick-to-act, imaginative, challenging, proud, bold, risk-taking, and so on, that is, in ways that when taken together suggest that the individual places the achievement of goals through influencing the activities of others at the top of his or her priorities in relating to others, we infer that his or her sense of self-worth comes from task accomplishment and the organization of resources toward that end.

> *An entrepreneurial business person, upon retirement, looks back over the years and feels fulfilled in the opportunities she uncovered and developed, the challenges she met and overcame, the loyalties she won and held, and the skills she had demonstrated in molding others into a successful, winning force.*

Analytic-Autonomizing (Green) Motivation. When an individual behaves in patterns of ways that can be characterized as cautious, practical, economical, reserved, methodical, analytic, principled, orderly, fair, persevering, conserving, thorough, and so on, that is, in ways that when taken together suggest that the individual places the achievement of self-reliance, self-sufficiency and self-dependence at the top of his or her priorities in relating to others, we infer that his or her sense of self-worth comes from the achievement of meaningful order.

> *A scientist, upon retirement, looks back over the years and expresses fulfillment in what she has been able to create, the order she has been able to bring out of chaos, the pursuit of excellence and, most importantly, her success in being her own person.*

Flexible-Cohering (Hub) Motivation. When an individual behaves in patterns that can be characterized as tolerant, flexible, social, adaptable, curious, open to change, negotiation, compromise, and so on, that is, in ways that when taken together suggest that the individual values flexibility and variety and often places being a good team member or team leader at the top of his or her priorities, we infer that this individual's sense of self-worth comes from the deployment of Blue, Red, or Green behaviors as the situation requires.

> *A police officer, upon retirement, looks back over the years and expresses fulfillment in the young people he has helped get on the right track, the protection he has provided to the elderly and the vulnerable, his arrests of offenders who have preyed on society, the establishment and maintenance of law and order in the face of crisis, his patient analysis of marginal clues, and his position as a trusted member of the team.*

Each of these orientations helps define the ways people behave based on their differing motivations. Motivations, however, may be mixed. People may act out of a combination of motivations. Relationship Awareness Theory defines these three possible combinations as well.

Assertive-Nurturing (Red-Blue) Motivation. These individuals are motivated by a desire to be both helpful and enterprising. These are often people who are quite assertive about bringing to others what they need.

> *A physician looks back over her career and sees as the greatest source of satisfaction the numerous opportunities she had to be of genuine help to others, often by having to be quite directive in getting people to do what she knew medically in her heart would be best for them.*

Judicious-Competing (Green-Red) Motivation. These individuals are motivated by a desire to be both enterprising and cautious. These people frequently use carefully thought-out strategies to accomplish their assertive objectives.

> *An attorney, at the end of his career, looks back over the years and sees as the greatest source of his satisfaction all the cases he had been able to win for his clients by using his ability to analyze information and present logical, forceful, persuasive arguments, to convince the judge and jury of the correctness of his point of view.*

Cautious-Supporting (Green-Blue) Motivation. These individuals are motivated by a desire to be both autonomous and helpful. These are people who will attempt to help others help themselves, but who will enter into those helping relationships with others only in so far as those relationships do not threaten their sense of autonomy.

> *A therapist, at the end of her career, looks back over the years and identifies as the major source of her satisfaction the occasions in which she had been able to be truly helpful to her patients and used her logical ability to analyze their problems and case histories while at the same time gaining new insights into the analytical skills required by her profession.*

Of course, everyone, under certain circumstances, wants to be of honest help to someone, wants to take charge and provide leadership and direction, wants to be left alone to figure things out for himself, and wants to remain flexible. Simply because someone is low on a particular scale, say the Blue scale, does not mean that he or she is never nurturant; it's just that this individual would be less frequently nurturant than someone who is higher on that scale. Almost no one is without some of each motivation, yet there is no doubt that most of us feel best about ourselves as people when we can behave in ways that are consistent with our primary orientation.

Interpreting your Scores on the Strength Deployment Inventory

On page four of the **Strength Deployment Inventory** you will find a chart titled "Points of Comparison between Patterns of Motivation." You might want to study that chart carefully as a way of further understanding your scores on the questionnaire. The following discussion is intended to supplement that chart.

> One note of caution: please bear in mind that "Points of Comparison between Patterns of Motivation" and the following discussion are describing individuals who are quite high on a given orientation. The higher your scores are on a particular orientation (and you have a scale of scores presented on page five of the **Strength Deployment Inventory**), the more likely a particular orientation will be characteristic of you. The lower your scores the less characteristic will be a particular description and the more you will find yourself combining information from more than one orientation to describe yourself.

You feel best about what you are doing when you are... This is the key concept in understanding each of the four orientations described in "Points of Comparison between Patterns of Motivation."

What is it that makes an individual feel good about himself or herself, that makes him or her feel authentic as a person—not at one given moment, but across the span of years?

For the Blue person, this sense of personal integrity is based upon the opportunities life affords to be genuinely helpful to others, with little or no expectation of or demand for any reward beyond clear evidence that he or she has been truly helpful.

> *We can think of the teacher whose gratifications stem from the number of kids who succeeded in life because of her. We think of the physician who is moved to tears when his efforts to save a life are successful and who pushes aside any thanks for his efforts as not due to him but to God, to the patient, to modern science—to any other cause but himself. We think of the husband who does something special for his wife and whose own enjoyment comes out of her enjoyment.*

The key to understanding this orientation is the drive to be genuinely—not superficially—helpful to others.

For the Red individual, the sense of personal worth is based upon his or her being a successful, winning leader of others. A missed opportunity is a failure. Competition is often the name of the game, and winning is the measure of the person. One cannot compete without the presence of a competitor. The bigger the game, the greater the need to rally the support of others in pursuit of the goal—achievement.

> *We need only think of the military leader who achieved the final victory by sheer grit, determination and force to catch the essence of this orientation. We can also think of the businessman or woman who seeks to rise to positions of authority, positions that are platforms for ever-widening influence, direction, and control. We can also go to any bookstore and scan the many books on leadership, sales, and corporate excellence, books which extoll the Red orientation as the heart of personal and professional success.*

The key to understanding this orientation is the drive to be a genuinely effective achiever in the face of competition.

For the Green individual the sense of personal integrity and authenticity arises out of a striving for self-sufficiency, self-reliance, and self-dependence, in short, out of a striving for autonomy. "Be your own person" is the name of the game; personal integrity is the measure of success. Fairness, not feelings. Principles, not power. These are the worthwhile goals.

> *Think of the engineers, the scientists, the scholars who would rather be right than popular, men and women whose greatest satisfactions in life come from the order they have been able to preserve or create, men and women who are rarely swayed by the persuasive arguments of others.*

The key to understanding this orientation is the drive to be self-reliant and self-sufficient.

For an individual in the Hub, the sense of personal worth and gratification lies in being the flexible person who can meet any contingency that may arise.

> *Think of the police officer who will risk his life to be helpful to someone in danger, who will exert force if the situation requires it, but who can be patient and even wise in settling a family dispute. Such a person can be nurturant, assertive, and analytic as required, but his or her sense of satisfaction comes from being able to adapt to a variety of different situations.*

The key to understanding this orientation is the need to be flexible.

You feel most rewarded by others when they treat you as... We all want to be successful, but what is success for one person is not success for another.

For the Blue person success is measured through the extent to which someone is truly helped. It is not enough just to help. To be fulfilling to the giver, the nurturance must have an effect. There must be evidence that the behavior meant to be helpful did indeed benefit someone. The child must show signs of having learned something new; the patient must show signs of restored health; the spouse must show signs of enjoyment. There must be evidence of the effectiveness of the nurturant behavior for the Blue person to experience success and a sense of personal fulfillment.

The Blue person, therefore, feels rewarded when others accept his or her help and express appreciation for that help.

The Red individual measures his or her success through the accomplishment of a challenging task. It is not enough just to lead and direct. To be fulfilled, this person must see his or her efforts result in tangible success. Evidence must exist for this individual that his or her direction has led to success, to having won, to being deserving of the right to provide leadership and direction.

The Red person, therefore, feels rewarded when others acknowledge and accept the results of his or her leadership.

The Green individual measures his or her success through the effective conservation of available resources, whether those resources are time, money, or energy. If the purchasing agent has bought it for less, he has conserved money. If the accountant plans her schedule, she has conserved time. If the engineer can design it more simply, he has saved time, money, and energy. To be fulfilled, this person must see evidence that his or her efforts have been logically and rationally correct.

The Green person, therefore, feels rewarded when others come to understand the logic and fairness of his or her actions.

A Hub measures his or her success by being able to do whatever is required at the moment. Regardless of what behavior is chosen, however, this person must see his or her efforts as having resulted in increased flexibility and, perhaps, group cooperation.

A Hub, therefore, feels rewarded when others treat him or her as a flexible individual, someone who can, when needed, be a valued member of the team.

You identify with and feel most at ease with people who...
The Blue person knows how important it is to be concerned for the welfare of others. This person understands the forgiveness of error, the giving of a second and a third chance, the giving of a Christmas bonus, the giving of praise. This person *knows* that nurturance of others is of the highest value because it produces human happiness and benefit. When this individual meets someone who shares these values, he or she is reassured as to how good and right these values are.

The Red person knows how productive the appropriate exercise of power and control can be. This person understands the need to give others a clear set of marching orders, to establish incentive systems, to set high standards of performance, to make decisions, to provide direction. This person *knows* that successful task accomplishment is of the highest value because it produces human happiness and achievement. When this individual meets someone who shares these values, he or she is reassured as to how good and right these values are.

The Green person knows how important it is to respect the integrity of others and the right of others to self-dependence. This person understands the need to give others time and space, to respect the opinions and ideas of others, to allow others to determine what is best for them. This individual *knows* that being one's own person is of the highest value because it produces certainty. When this individual meets someone who shares these values, he or she is reassured as to how good and right these values are.

A Hub knows how important it is to be flexible and understands the value of keeping his or her options open, of adapting, of variety. This person *knows* that being flexible and responsive is of the highest value. When this individual meets someone who shares these values, he or she is reassured as to how good and right these values are.

You are attracted to and intrigued by others who are...and ideally you would like to be... These two items go together because most people would occasionally like to be more like those whose orientation is different.

The Blue person, wanting to be genuinely helpful, will be attracted to those who are strong and know exactly what they want to do. As long as the other person knows what he or she wants to do, the Blue person is in a position to know how to be helpful. And when others want them to be included in their activities and successes, the Blue person is assured that his or her help is wanted and valued. Ideally, Blues would like to be more assertive and more frequently able to stop people from imposing on them.

The Red person, wanting to provide leadership, will be attracted to those who want to help him or her achieve success. The nurturant follower can provide an awareness of others' feelings, while the analytic follower can provide an awareness of others' rights. Ideally, Reds would like to be more sensitive to other people and more thoughtful and careful before taking action.

The Green person, valuing self-reliance, self-sufficiency and self-dependence, will be attracted to others who make their wants and feelings known, but who do not impose those wants and feelings on him or her. Green individuals, who frequently would like to be more open and less reserved about pushing for what they want, feel attracted to others who can be decisive and explicit about what they want and how they feel. Ideally, Greens would like to be both more trusting and more assertive.

The Hub person will find highly nurturant, highly assertive, and highly analytic people intriguing because each has something to offer. By becoming better at being Blue and Red and Green, the Hub can become a more completely flexible person.

Ideally, you would like to avoid ever being... The Blue person wants to avoid ever being selfish, cold, or unfeeling, for others would then not count on him or her for help and support.

The Red person wants to avoid ever being gullible or indecisive, for if one is gullible, the other person might take advantage and win, while if one is indecisive, nothing gets accomplished.

The Green person wants to avoid ever being controlled by his or her emotions or so lacking in respect for others as to take advantage of them or exploit them. To be emotional is the opposite of being rational; to exploit others is a violation of one's own sense of integrity.

A Hub wants to avoid ever being subservient, domineering, or isolated, for in so doing he or she might lose his or her flexibility or limit his or her options.

You feel distant from and somewhat contemptuous of people who…and you feel acute discomfort from people who…
These two items go together because each identifies people that cause some difficulty for particular orientations.

Blue people, valuing being helpful, tend to look with contempt on people they view as personally competitive and exploitative, and on people they see as cold and unresponsive. Blues will feel threatened by any form of clear rejection of their willingness to be helpful.

Red people, valuing competition and task accomplishment, tend to be contemptuous of people they see as losers, and of people they see as so reserved that they will not compete. Reds will feel threatened by anyone who will not join the argument or by those who don't say what they want.

Green people, valuing self-reliance and self-dependence, will tend to be contemptuous of people they see as offering unasked-for help, and of people they see as being overly persuasive or forceful. Greens will feel threatened by any situation that requires them to be dependent on others.

A Hub, often valuing membership in the group, will tend to be contemptuous of those who reject the group in any way, and of those whom they see as meeting every problem with the same set of answers. Hubs will feel threatened by anything which cuts off their options or takes away the opportunity to be flexible.

Every Person is Like No Other Person

By now you should have a fairly good idea of what your scores on the **Strength Deployment Inventory** mean for you when things are going well. As you have read these various descriptions, however, you have probably found that not everything characteristic of your orientation applied to you, while you probably noted certain characteristics of other orientations that applied to you as well. Even though we are all like each other in that we all seek to interact with others in ways that make us feel good about ourselves as people, and even though we are all like some other people in that we can be described as Blues, Reds, Greens, or Hubs, every person is like *no other person* in that each of us puts these strengths together in our own unique ways.

To help you get a sense of how you put these strengths together, I would like to ask you to complete an exercise that will help you identify your characteristic strengths. On the form below, first rate each of the listed ways of behaving from 0 to 3 as to how much it is like you to use that particular strength. Please use the scale provided at the top of the form.

Identify your Characteristic Strengths:
3-Very much like you; 2-Quite a bit like you; 1-Somewhat like you; 0-Not like you

Blue		**Red**		**Green**		**Hub**	
Trusting		Self-Confident		Cautious		Flexible	
Optimistic		Enterprising		Practical		Open to change	
Loyal		Ambitious		Economical		Socializer	
Idealistic		Organizing		Reserved		Experimenter	
Helpful		Persuasive		Methodical		Curious	
Modest		Forceful		Analytic		Adaptable	
Devoted		Quick to act		Principled		Tolerant	
Caring		Imaginative		Orderly		Open to Compromise	
Supportive		Competitive		Fair		Looks for Options	
Accepting		Proud		Persevering		Socially sensitive	
Polite		Bold		Conserving		Team player	
Undemanding		Risk-taking		Thorough		Mediator	

Next, please circle the six ways of behaving that you believe are most characteristic of you. Then, list those six ways of behaving in the spaces provided below in order from most to least characteristic of you. Finally, identify after each of those six strengths how or in what way that behavior is a strength for you.

The six strengths most like me are:

Strength	How this is a strength for me
1. _____	_____
2. _____	_____
3. _____	_____
4. _____	_____
5. _____	_____
6. _____	_____

As you look at that list of six strengths, do you find that many of them come from your primary orientation? Do you notice that one or more of those strengths are from other orientations? (You may, of course, have taken all six from a single orientation, but that is relatively rare.)

Every person is indeed like no other person, for we all combine these strengths in our own unique ways. It is quite possible for two people to have exactly the same scores on columns one, two, and three of the **Strength Deployment Inventory** and yet have quite different profiles of strengths. Relationship Awareness Theory can be a very powerful way of learning about ourselves and each other. At the same time the theory shows us how each of us is unique and different.

Conclusion

No orientation on the **Strength Deployment Inventory** is in-herently superior to another orientation except in the eye of the beholder. Each of us, at some time or another, wants to be genuinely nurturant of another human being. For some, this want fills a large part of our lives and is characteristic of our relationships with others. Who is to say that this orientation is better than the others? It is simply so, and when the opportunity presents itself to help others, we do so and do not condemn ourselves for wanting to be of help.

Each of us, at some time or another, wants to step in, take the lead and organize and direct the activity of others. For some of us, this want fills a large part of our lives and dominates our relationships with others. Who is to say that this orientation is better than the others? It is simply so, and when the chance presents itself to lead, we do so and do not condemn ourselves for wanting to provide direction.

Each of us, at some time or another, wants to pursue something in our own way, at our own pace and independently of others. For some of us, this want fills a large part of our lives and is characteristic of our relationships with others. Who is to say that this orientation is better than the others? It is simply so, and when the chance presents itself to be our own person, we do so and do not condemn ourselves for wanting to be autonomous.

Each of us, at some time or another, wants to be flexible and open to various options or to the needs of the group. For some of us, this want fills a large part of our lives and dominates our relationships with others. Who is to say that this orientation is better than the others? It is simply so, and when the chance presents itself to maintain our flexibility, we do so and do not condemn ourselves for wanting to be a good team member.

Again, no one orientation is inherently superior to another orientation except in the eye of the beholder. However, as we shall come to see, *most of us act as though our own particular orientation were the only reasonable way to be*, and therein lies the basis for the difficulty we have all experienced in human relations. We'll begin looking at one aspect of that difficulty in the next chapter as we explore the ways our strengths can become our weaknesses.

Examples

Page 12. Someone with high scores on the Blue scale might answer these statements in the following manner:

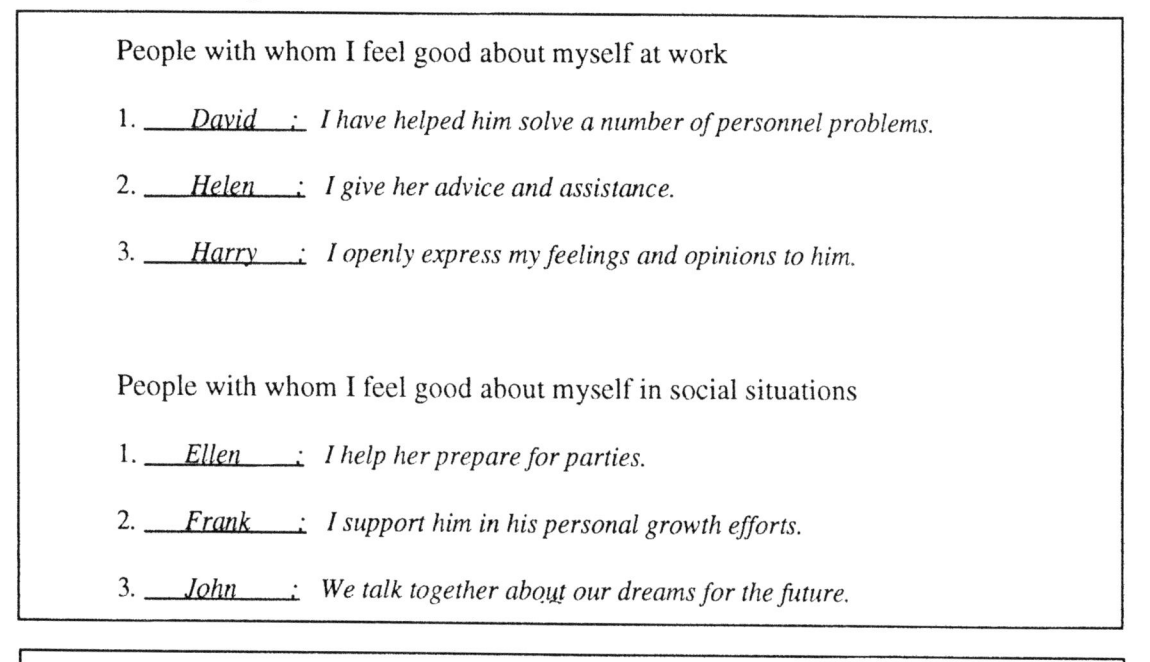

People with whom I feel good about myself at work

1. __*David*__ : *I have helped him solve a number of personnel problems.*

2. __*Helen*__ : *I give her advice and assistance.*

3. __*Harry*__ : *I openly express my feelings and opinions to him.*

People with whom I feel good about myself in social situations

1. __*Ellen*__ : *I help her prepare for parties.*

2. __*Frank*__ : *I support him in his personal growth efforts.*

3. __*John*__ : *We talk together about our dreams for the future.*

I most enjoy a relationship in which I can be

close to other people, working with them and helping them.

Chapter Two

Page 23. Someone with high scores on the Red scale might answer these statements as follows:

The six strengths most like me are:

Strength	How this is a strength for me
1. *Self-confidence*	*helps me carry out my ideas in the face of opposition*
2. *Imaginative*	*helps me be more creative and solve problems others see as impossible*
3. *Persuasive*	*essential to getting my ideas carried out by others*
4. *Methodical*	*helps me carry out my ideas in an efficient manner*
5. *Supportive*	*helps me help others in the group to achieve our objectives under stress*
6. *Fair*	*balances my enthusiasm by helping me listen to the ideas of others*

Chapter Three

Understanding Weaknesses

A personal weakness is no more or less than an overdoing of a personal strength. In this chapter we look at this important idea in greater detail.

When we behave toward another person in ways that help both of us feel good about ourselves, we operate out of a position of strength and create a "win-win" relationship. To be trusting in a relationship when trust is called for, to be self-confident in a relationship in which self-confidence is called for, to be fair in a relationship in which fairness is called for, to be flexible when flexibility is called for — these are all strengths and help to build mutually productive relationships.

On the other hand, when we overdo a strength or use a strength in situations where it is not appropriate, that strength can become a weakness and thus lead to the creation of a "lose-lose" relationship. To be over-trusting or gullible is a weakness, for it lessens the likelihood of mutual gratification and invites the other party to exploit the relationship or to withdraw. To be over-confident or arrogant is a weakness, for it lessens the likelihood of mutual gratification and invites hostility or withdrawal from the other person. To be overly cautions or suspicious is a weakness, for it lessens the likelihood of mutual gratification and creates lack of trust or withdrawal in the other person. To be overly flexible or unpredictable is a weakness, for it lessens the likelihood of mutual gratification and creates only confusion.

Besides a "win-win" and a "lose-lose" relationship there is of course is a "win-lose" relationship. Relationship Awareness Theory sees this as a "lose-lose" relationship. Although in the short term the "winner" in a "win-lose" relationship may seem to be benefiting from that relationship, in the long term that relationship, even if it survives (which is not likely), will be destructive for both parties.

Identifying the Strengths You May Overdo

Each of your strengths has the capacity of becoming a weakness. In Chapter Two you identified several of your characteristic strengths, and you might want to review those strengths at this point. Now, look over the following chart, in which those strengths have been paired with their corresponding weaknesses and circle the half-dozen or so strengths that you may overdo.

Chapter Three

Strengths You May Overdo

Blue	Red	Green	Hub
Trusting *Gullible*	Self-Confident *Arrogant*	Cautious *Suspicious*	Flexible *Inconsistent*
Optimistic *Impractical*	Enterprising *Opportunistic*	Practical *Unimaginative*	Open to change *Wishy-washy*
Loyal *Slavish*	Ambitious *Ruthless*	Economical *Stingy*	Socializer *Can't be alone*
Idealistic *Wishful*	Organizer *Controller*	Reserved *Cold*	Experimenter *Aimless*
Helpful *Self-denying*	Persuasive *Pressuring*	Methodical *Rigid*	Curious *Nosy*
Modest *Self-effacing*	Forceful *Dictatorial*	Analytic *Nit-picking*	Adaptable *Spineless*
Devoted *Self-sacrificing*	Quick to act *Rash*	Principled *Unbending*	Tolerant *Uncaring*
Caring *Smothering*	Imaginative *Dreamer*	Orderly *Compulsive*	Open to Compromise *No principles*
Supportive *Submissive*	Competitive *Combative*	Fair *Unfeeling*	Looks for Options *No focus*
Accepting *Passive*	Proud *Conceited*	Persevering *Stubborn*	Socially sensitive *Dependent*
Polite *Deferential*	Bold *Brash*	Conserving *Possessive*	Team player *Groupie*
Undemanding *Masochistic*	Risk-taking *Gambler*	Thorough *Obsessive*	Mediator *No convictions*

Costs of Overdoing Strengths

Now, let's look at the costs to you of overdoing those strengths. List in the space provided below your most frequently overdone strengths. Then, in the space provided next to each strength, describe how people tend to react to that overdone strength. Essentially, you are being asked to put yourself in someone else's place for a moment and to recall from past experiences their response to your overdone strengths.

The three strengths I am most likely to overdo:

Overdone strength	How others respond to my overdone strength
1. _____	_____
	_____
2. _____	_____
	_____
3. _____	_____
	_____

Can you see that this idea of a weakness as being nothing more than an inappropriate use of a strength is one of the most revealing concepts in Relationship Awareness Theory? Think of your own strengths. Things go well for you when you use those strengths appropriately. Then, suddenly or gradually, you become aware of the fact that, once again, you have gone too far. Instead of using a strength you have over done it or used it in a situation in which it was no longer appropriate.

To become more aware of the ways you may run into problems, look over the following ten sure ways to overdo a strength, paying particular attention to your own primary orientation when things are going well.

Expectations

You will frequently over-do your orientation if you consistently expect others to:

Blue	Red	Green	Hub
Value friendship and harmony first and foremost.	Value competition and rivalry first and foremost.	Value facts and principles first and foremost.	Value flexibility and togetherness first and foremost.
Want your help.	Want to follow you.	Be logical and keep feelings under control.	Be sensitive to what the situation calls for.
Be guided by feelings and concern for feelings.	Trust your judgement without questioning it.	Want your logical analysis and judgement.	Want you to develop as many options as possible.
Treat you warmly and with affection.	Treat you with admiration and envy.	Treat you with reason and respect.	Treat you as a valued resource person.
Make your decisions for you.	Make rapid and incisive decisions.	Make only considered decisions.	Make decisions by consensus.

Impositions

You are imposing your values on others when:

Blue	Red	Green	Hub
You press your help on others who don't need your help.	You tell only part of the story in order to get your own way.	You withdraw from others without any explanation.	You stick your nose in where it's not wanted.
You press your help on others who don't want your help.	You press your way on others who don't want to do it your way.	You insist that others be independent of you when they don't want to be.	You insist on looking at yet one more option.
Your mission is to help the needy no matter at what cost.	Your mission is to get the job done at any cost.	Your mission is to think things through and let the chips fall where they may.	Your mission is idea-generation, not commitment.
Harmony is more important to you than facing issues or facts.	Winning is more important than feelings or facts.	Facts and principles are more important than feelings or what others want to do.	Group choesiveness is more important than group goals.
You act to please others just to be likeable.	You act to direct others just to assert your authority.	You act to turn others away just to assert your independence.	You act to bring others together just because you want togetherness.

At this point, if not at some earlier point in this chapter or this book, you may have begun to contemplate the possibility of changing some of the behavior you have identified through the **Strength Deployment Inventory**. Let me make a couple of suggestions for you about that possibility.

First, it does happen that some people find themselves either not liking some of the things they have found out about themselves through the inventory or wishing they could make additional strengths more readily available. The question then arises, "Can I change my scores?" The answer is, "Yes, it is possible to manipulate your scores on each of the twenty items in any way you decide. However, your first response to these items is a reflection of the basic purpose or motivation of your behavior. Your initial assignment of numbers to each item reflects what you find satisfying in human relations. Your unique, preferred way of relating to others was established early in your life. Your initial scores on the **Strength Deployment Inventory** indicate where you get your fundamental satisfaction in interaction with others."

Second, what is important and possible is not changing your *scores* on the **Strength Deployment Inventory** but becoming more skillful in *using the behaviors identified by those scores.* What you may have found yourself not liking about your scores is not the behavior they describe when things are going well but instead the trouble you find yourself getting into when those strengths are overdone. It is possible to monitor your behavior so that you can guard against overdoing those strengths.

To help you in doing that, please identify three things you might begin doing right now to reduce the frequency with which you overdo your strengths.

---

1. The first thing I could do to reduce the frequency with which I overdo my strengths would be to _____

2. The second thing I could do to reduce the frequency with which I overdo my strengths would be to _____

3. The third thing I could do to reduce the frequency with which I overdo my strengths would be to _____

Human relationships become puzzling when we find others reacting negatively to us (from our point of view) for no apparent reason. Relationship Awareness Theory suggests that we may indeed be the cause of that problem. With our best intentions, one of our most cherished strengths has become a weakness. Of course, because we have overdone that strength with the best of intentions, we usually find it easy to forgive ourselves. Others, however, may find forgiveness more difficult! It is far better to be aware at the outset of the ways in which our strengths may get us into trouble than to try to patch up a relationship after the damage has been done.

Things You May Need To Be On Guard Against

As we have seen, each strength brings with it a potential weakness. Consequently, as the foregoing table suggests, there are things each orientation needs to be on guard against.

BLUE	RED	GREEN	HUB
Wanting so much to maintain harmony that I don't push for what I want.	Wanting so much to win that I step on others to get my own way.	Wanting so much to be certain that I delay in reaching decisions.	Wanting so much to be flexible that I am sometimes inconsistent.
Being so quick to believe in others that I don't use good judgment.	Being in such a hurry to get things done that I disregard how others feel about things.	Being so concerned with what is right and/or wrong that I pay little attention to people's feelings.	Being so open-minded that I lose sight of what I really think.
Being so loyal to others that I let them take advantage of me.	Being so sure I am right that I don't listen to other people.	Being so cautious that I find it hard to place trust in others.	Needing to be with others so much I find it hard to be alone.
Expecting everyone to be as concerned about how others feel as I do.	Expecting everyone to enjoy competing with me and pushing for what they want.	Expecting everyone to be as concerned as I am with details, logic, and principle.	Expecting everyone to be as concerned as I am with being a good team member.
Wanting to help others so much that I push my help on them and get in their way.	Wanting others to do things my way so much I become dictatorial.	Wanting to be so self-dependent that I cut myself off from people who really like and can help me.	Wanting to "fit in" so much that I impress others as having no real convictions.
Being quick to blame myself first for anything that goes wrong.	Being quick to blame anything that goes wrong on the failure of others to cooperate.	Being quick to blame anything that goes wrong on my not having been cautious enough.	Being quick to blame anything that goes wrong on a lack of teamwork.
Sharing my thoughts and feelings with people I shouldn't trust with them.	Sharing only those thoughts and feelings that help me get my own way.	Keeping my thoughts and feelings about myself to myself so others don't get to know me.	Accepting other people's thoughts and feelings in place of my own.
Fearing that if I said what I really feel about others, they would be hurt and not helped.	Fearing that if I said what I really feel, others would know how to take advantage of me.	Fearing that if I said what I really feel, others would see me as illogical and emotional.	Fearing that if I said what I really feel, others would see me as being rigid.
Struggling to maintain harmony at the expense of facing the facts.	Struggling to win an issue regardless of what the facts are or what others might feel.	Struggling with the facts and issues with such determination that others' feelings are ignored.	Struggling so hard to keep my options open I never take a clear line of action.
Acting to please others just to be likeable.	Acting to direct others just to exert my authority.	Acting to turn others away just to assert my self-dependence.	Acting to disagree with others just to show there are many ways to do things.

Conclusion

Being trusting to the point of being gullible, being self-confident to the point of being arrogant, being cautious to the point of being suspicious, these are examples of strengths that are actually overdone. But what happens when, for example, a Red interacts with a Blue? When that Red acts with self-confidence, ambition, and directness, the highly nurturant person may well perceive him or her as arrogant, aggressive, overbearing and rash. In other words, not only can we actually overdo a strength but we can sometimes be seen by others of differing orientations as overdoing a strength when in our own estimation we are not.

A fact of human relations, made clear through Relationship Awareness Theory, is that individuals of one orientation are apt to judge much of the behavior of individuals of other orientations as being overdone. We need to take this into account in our own perceptions of others and to understand that people of different orientations may see us much less favorably than we see ourselves.

To make matters worse, whether or not a strength is really being overdone is often a matter of both judgment and hindsight. For example, if a Blue has reason to trust someone deeply, that Blue will seldom be talked out of trusting but will perhaps be angered by others who say he or she is being gullible. If that trust turns out to be justified, the Blue person's behavior has been vindicated. If the trust turns out to have been badly placed, then and only then can the Blue person see that he or she has been gullible.

Each of us can be responsible only for our own behavior and not for the responses that others might have to our behavior. If as a Red, for instance, you choose to act in a self-confident and assertive manner, you cannot be responsible if others see you as arrogant and controlling. On the other hand, if you are aware of the ways your Red strengths at times get you into difficulty, you are in a position to manage your behavior so that you foster amicable relations with others. This insight into self-management is one of the most profound and useful contributions Relationship Awareness Theory can make to human relations.

Chapter Three

Examples

Page 29. A Hub might complete these activities as follows:

The three strengths I am most likely to overdo:

Overdone strength	How others respond to my overdone strength
1. *Flexible*	*tends to be seen by others as being inconsistent, as not taking a stand*
2. *Experimenter*	*people rightly see my jumping from interest to interest as aimlessness*
3. *Fair*	*I can appear to be unfeeling because I sometimes ignore others' emotions*

Page 31. This same Hub might complete these statements as follows:

1. The first thing I could do to reduce the frequency with which I overdo my strengths would be to

be more aware of the need to take a position on important issues. I do need to look at all sides of the question, but I also need to make up my mind sooner than I sometimes do.

2. The second thing I could do to reduce the frequency with which I overdo my strengths would be to

stick with it and to keep myself from being sidetracked by interesting but, at least for the moment, not very relevant issues.

3. The third thing I could do to reduce the frequency with which I overdo my strengths would be to

*let people know that I **do** hear their feelings, even if sometimes, in my need to be fair, I appear somewhat cold.*

Chapter Four

Understanding Conflict

In the first two chapters you explored in some detail the way you deploy your strengths when things are going well for you, when you are free to pursue those goals and activities that help you feel good about yourself as a person. I am sure, however, that there have been times when you have found yourself experiencing some sort of conflict or opposition, in which things are not going well for you. Relationship Awareness Theory can help us understand and even cope with these difficulties as we now begin to explore the nature of interpersonal conflict.

To help understand conflict, think of someone you find difficult or puzzling. This could be someone from either your personal or professional life, but think of someone with whom you frequently find yourself in disagreement, someone who is in some way a problem for you, at least part of the time. To clarify your thinking about that person, and to give you an example which can be used later, provide the following information.

---

1. First, describe the nature of this difficult or puzzling relationship when things are going well for you. In general, what is going on in that relationship that makes it so difficult?

   _____

   _____

   _____

2. What specifically is it that the other person does to give you a problem or cause you difficulties?

   _____

   _____

   _____

3. When that happens, what is the first thing you usually do? How do you usually react when you experience this particular kind of difficulty with that person?

_____

_____

_____

4. Once you have done that, how does the other person usually respond?

_____

_____

_____

5. Once the other person has responded in this way, what do you do? Do you continue with the behavior described in number three above, or does your behavior tend to change? If so, how does it change?

_____

_____

_____

As you read through the following discussion of conflict, please keep this relationship and your description of what happens in mind. You may want to come back to these descriptions to make additional notes or comments as you begin to use Relationship Awareness Theory to understand more about the nature of interpersonal conflict.

Unwarranted Conflict

There are basically two kinds of conflict. The first is what Relationship Awareness Theory describes as "unwarranted conflict." By this is simply meant conflict that need not exist. Unwarranted conflict occurs between individuals whose motivation patterns differ and who are apparently unaware of those differences. More often than not, the way each person behaves is simply not understandable to the other because neither would behave as the other does. Consider the following relationship as an example of unwarranted conflict.

> *Alice Thompson was the Training Director of a major urban hospital. Her highest score when things were going well was Green. Phyllis Appleby, the Director of Nursing for the hospital, was Red. Both individuals, in quite different ways, however, were committed to making the hospital as effective as possible.*
>
> *During one meeting, attended by Alice and several other senior administrators of the hospital, Phyllis began to present a plan for the recruitment, training and utilization of nurses, a plan which she represented as novel and certain to cut down on personnel turnover. In a manner quite characteristic of high scorers on the Red scale, she placed her greatest emphasis upon the goals to be accomplished, the advantages to be gained, the opportunities to be seized upon, the challenges to be faced and overcome, and the need for leadership in successfully completing this effort.*
>
> *Alice Thompson, in a manner quite characteristic of people with high scores on the Green scale, began to be concerned with just how Phyllis intended to make all these good things come true. She felt she needed to reserve judgement until she had learned just how Phyllis intended to implement her plan. She began asking questions intended to get at the logic of how this project would proceed. She counseled the need for caution in presuming that the program would have instant success. She asked detailed questions about what she saw the role of training to be in the program.*
>
> *It was not very long before Phyllis turned on her and with evident hostility accused Alice of being "nit-picking" and "uncooperative." Alice in turn felt hurt, rejected, and, most of all, deeply puzzled as to why her legitimate concern over*

logical procedure should be met with such hostility. What had started off as two people trying to achieve a common goal had ended in conflict.

I would like to ask you to put your knowledge of Relationship Awareness Theory to work in understanding this relationship by answering the following three questions:

1. As a Red, what was Phyllis Appleby trying to accomplish with her plan?

2. As a Green, what was Alice Thompson trying to do in responding to Phyllis' ideas?

3. What was the cause of the unwarranted conflict the two were experiencing in this situation?

Phyllis, as a Red, was of course primarily concerned with goal or task accomplishment. She was excited about the challenge to be faced and was feeling good about herself as someone able to provide the leadership and enthusiasm needed to meet that challenge. As Reds sometimes do, however, she had not thought through very carefully all the details of implementation that would need to be addressed if her plan were ever to be achieved.

Alice, as a Green, was of course concerned with orderliness and thoroughness, with what is practical, logical, and, above all, realistic. As Greens often do, however, she was unaware of how dampening these concerns could be to someone like Phyllis. The more Alice questioned Phyllis' plans, and the more Phyllis pushed back at Alice, the less opportunity each had to feel good about themselves and each other.

In a training session on Relationship Awareness Theory shortly after this meeting, Alice came to understand this basic difference between her valued relating style and that of Phyllis. On the basis of understanding what *she* was striving for and how that differed from what *Phyllis* was striving for, she designed a strategy to meet both her needs and Phyllis'.

> *At the next staff meeting Phyllis continued her presentation of her project with a continued emphasis upon the successful achievement of program goals. As difficult as it was, Alice managed to keep quiet during the presentation and simply made notes to herself regarding various procedural problems she saw in the plan. When Phyllis had completed her presentation and was ready for questions, Alice began with this question: "Phyllis, I'm not sure at what level you want me to react to your ideas. Do you want me to comment on whether or not I feel the goals you are after are worthwhile and worth pursuing? Or would you rather I comment on some of the problems that I see will have to be solved if we are going to achieve those goals?"*
>
> *Phyllis looked at Alice for several moments in stunned silence before responding with an enthusiastic "Both! First, I'd like your evaluation as to whether or not you feel I'm heading in the right direction. And then, if you do agree on what it is I want to accomplish, I'd love to have your help on thinking through how to proceed." At this point, the two began working together in greater harmony, in mutual respect, and in mutual acceptance of their differences.*

Through her understanding of Relationship Awareness Theory, Alice was able to manage the situation in such a way that both she and Phyllis could work together in ways that enhanced their self-worth and valued each others' strengths.

Managing Unwarranted Conflict

Whenever a Blue acts upon and expresses a primary concern for the welfare of others, that person risks being seen by Reds as a loser, as weak, and as being too concerned with making people happy. That same Blue risks being seen by Greens, however, as overly emotional, as one who puts feeling before fact, as wasteful and idealistic.

Whenever a Red acts upon and expresses a primary concern for task accomplishment, that person risks being seen by Blues as pushy, dictatorial, bossy, and even ruthless. That same Red risks being seen by Greens, however, as rash, hurried, unthinking, and even power-hungry.

Whenever a Green expresses a primary concern about thinking things through in a logical manner and reserving judgment until all the facts are in, that person risks being seen by Blues as cold, unfeeling, uncaring, untouchable, and lonely. That same Green risks being seen by Reds as rigid, paralyzed, stingy and unimaginative.

Hubs, of course, see Blues, Reds and Greens as all right part of the time but as too apt to go overboard, to be inflexible and unresponsive to the demands of the situation.

Whenever a Hub, on the other hand, acts upon and expresses a primary concern for keeping all available options open so that he or she can respond appropriately to whatever the situation calls for at the moment, that person risks being seen by Blues as confusing and unpredictable, by Reds as inconsistent and distracted, and by Greens as spineless and unprincipled.

Although unwarranted conflict is very common and can sometimes go on for years, there are several things we can do to reduce the occurrence of this kind of conflict and thus help create win-win relationships.

First, do not assume that the other person is operating out of the same valued relating style as you. We all want to feel good about ourselves as human beings, but what makes you feel good about yourself may be quite different from what makes the other person feel good.

Second, become more aware of the orientation of the other person. Since others may be operating out of a different valued relating style than yours, become aware of the fact that the valued relating style can bring strengths to the relationship that you do not possess. Learn to build on those strengths in creating a mutually productive relationship.

Third, avoid overdoing your strengths. As we have seen, each orientation tends to see the orientation of the other as being overdone. The harder you push your strengths, the more opportunity you are providing the other to see your strengths as weaknesses and thus creating unwarranted conflict.

Fourth, be sure you are providing the other person with enough opportunities to get what he or she wants out of a relationship. Be aware of what brings the other person a sense of self-worth and what takes it away.

Fifth, do not devalue the other person's valued relating style. This is for many of us very hard to do, since in our heart of hearts we *know* that our orientation is the best. As difficult as it may be, however, we simply must learn to accept the fact that there are different ways of being in the world and that those ways are as equally valuable as our own.

At this point, you might want to return to the notes you made at the beginning of this chapter and to explore the ways in which the problems in that relationship may be the result of unwarranted conflict. You may wish to use the space on the next page to record your reflections.

In what ways does the concept of unwarranted conflict help you to understand the difficult relationship you described at the beginning of this chapter?

Not all conflicts, however, are unwarranted. To gain a deeper understanding of the nature of interpersonal conflict, we must now turn to the second kind of conflict described by Relationship Awareness Theory.

Real Conflict

The second kind of conflict occurs when you encounter a situation that makes it impossible to achieve that which you find gratifying. This may happen when you find yourself unable to resolve unwarranted conflict. What would have happened, for instance, to Phyllis if she had continued to encounter the kind of opposition she first experienced from Alice? At some point, that unwarranted conflict would have become quite real for her, for she would no longer be able to behave in ways that helped her feel good about herself as a person.

Conflict is generated by a relationship or situation in which a person is blocked from expressing his or her primary valued relating style. How would a Blue feel if his help were rejected or unneeded? How would a Red feel if no one would follow her? How would a Green feel if she were unable to maintain a sense of self-dependence or autonomy? How would a Hub feel if he were unable to keep his options open for as long as he might like? In these and similar situations we find ourselves experiencing real conflict or opposition.

Conflict and stress, however, are not necessarily the same. Although conflict may indeed be stressful, the fact that we are experiencing stress at any given moment does not necessarily mean that we are also experiencing conflict.

> *As part of a training program for dealing with emergencies in a major power plant, it was decided to assign people to handle jobs that were compatible with their scores on the* **Strength Deployment Inventory** *under conflict. It was assumed that emergency conditions were equivalent to conflict because they were stressful.*
>
> *As the training program was implemented, however, it was discovered that, under emergency conditions, people tended to assume roles consistent with their primary (when things are going well) orientation on the* **Strength Deployment Inventory***.*

Stress occurs when you are pushed, and you may at times experience stress in implementing your primary orientation. *Conflict exists only when you are cut off from the opportunity to behave in ways that increase your feelings of self-worth.*

Think about your own experience with conflict. When you find yourself unable to express your primary orientation, what's your first response? What if that response doesn't seem to work? Have you ever noticed yourself shifting to another response? What was it? Have you ever been in a situation or relationship in which, in spite of your best efforts, the conflict continued on and on? Have you ever felt totally pushed to the wall, as if you were absolutely out of options? What did you do then?

This sequence of responses that you probably have gone through many, many times is the key to understanding the way all of us deal with conflict or opposition. Let's look at that sequence now in more detail.

Strength Deployment in the Face of Conflict or Opposition

When things are going well for you, you characteristically deploy your strengths *simultaneously*, in a predictable, uniform and consistent way. Look at your scores from the **Strength Deployment Inventory** in columns one, two, and three. When things are going well for you, all of the behaviors identified by those three numbers are available to you simultaneously as your valued relating style. You may *use one or more* of these strengths more frequently than the others, but they're all available to you at the same moment.

Chapter Four

The longer your arrow on the triangle on page five of the **Strength Deployment Inventory**, the more dramatic will this shift be. The longer the arrow, the greater the shift in behavior and the more quickly others will become aware of the fact that you are experiencing conflict.

When faced with conflict or opposition, however, you no longer deploy your strengths simultaneously but instead shift to a *sequential* or *serial* deployment. You become what Relationship Awareness Theory calls "predictably variable," which simply means that it is possible to predict the way you vary your responses in the face of conflict. To follow that shift, write in below your scores from columns four, five, and six from the **Strength Deployment Inventory**, which show the sequence you go through when you encounter conflict or opposition.

Column Four	Column Five	Column Six

These responses to real conflict are best understood as attempts to preserve your sense of self-worth and integrity. You feel most worthwhile about yourself when you are free to pursue your primary orientation. Real conflict prevents you from doing that and thus, when you face real conflict, you are to some extent no longer able to feel worthwhile about yourself. Your responses to real conflict are attempts to get back, figuratively, to page one of the **Strength Deployment Inventory** so that you can continue to feel the sense of self-worth associated with your scores when things are going well for you.

We can think of dealing with conflict or opposition as taking place in three stages. The first response is to try to brush the conflict aside. Our intent here is simply to make the conflict go away so as not to jeopardize our unobstructed pursuit of our basic orientation. If this doesn't work, we shift to our second level of dealing with conflict, which involves preserving our sense of self-worth in the face of continuing opposition. If this in turn doesn't work, as a last resort we shift once again to our final response to conflict and opposition. The further you progress through this sequence the worse you feel about yourself as a person.

There are thirteen possible ways of combining scores in the face of conflict or opposition. To understand the way you go about dealing with conflict, find the *one* description below that fits your scores in columns four, five and six.

You are, of course, free to read the descriptions of how others with different scores respond to conflict, but the primary concern here is that you understand *your* behavior in the face of conflict, not others'. If you do read these descriptions straight through, expect to find them, taken together, as boring and repetitious.

If your scores in columns four, five and six are all at least seven or more points apart, one of the following six descriptions will apply to you.

> Scores that are six or less points apart on the **Strength Deployment Inventory** should be treated as statistically equal.

1. Your highest score is Blue, your second highest score is Red, and your lowest score is Green. Your first response to conflict or opposition is most likely to be disbelief that conflict exists. You may feel that everything will be all right, that there is some simple misunderstanding that can be cleared up. You probably go a bit out of your way to be nice because, after all, if you're nice enough, the conflict will fade away. You will tend to experience your behavior as simply being accommodating to the needs of others. And you will continue to feel this way until it dawns on you that the conflict or opposition has not disappeared at all.

At this point, you will have come to the conclusion that the battle must be joined and you will tend to experience your behavior as having to fight off the opposition. But if this doesn't work, your last stand behavior will be to finally break off the relationship and, if your scores are ten or lower in the Green, you will tend to experience your behavior as a complete retreat.

2. Your highest score is Blue, your second highest score is Green, and your lowest score is Red. Your first response to conflict or opposition is most likely to be disbelief that conflict exists. You may feel that everything will be all right, that there is some simple misunderstanding that can be cleared up. You probably go a bit out of your way to be nice because, after all, if you're nice enough, the conflict will fade away. You will tend to experience your behavior as simply being accommodating to the needs of others. And you will continue to feel this way until it dawns on you that the conflict or opposition has not disappeared at all.

At this point you will probably try to protect your autonomy by backing off, defending yourself against any further intrusion and preserving whatever integrity you have left. You will tend to experience your behavior as trying to escape from the opposition. But if this doesn't work, your last stand behavior will be to finally fight for your rights and, if your scores are ten or lower in the Red, you will tend to experience your behavior as having to fight for your life, sometimes in very explosive ways.

3. Your highest score is Red, your second highest score is Blue, and your lowest score is Green. Your first response to conflict or opposition is most apt to be some form of challenge, some kind of "fighting off" behavior. You probably would experience the other person as being wrong and certainly not entitled to make you give up what you want to do. You will tend to experience your behavior as simply rising to the challenge that is being offered. And you will continue to feel this way until it dawns on you that trying to "fight off" the conflict is not going to make it go away.

At this point, you are most apt to go out of your way to be accommodating to the other person. You will tend to experience your behavior as giving in and letting the opposition have its way. If this doesn't work, your last stand behavior will be to finally break off the relationship and, if your scores are ten or lower in the Green, you will tend to experience your behavior as a complete retreat.

4. Your highest score is Red, your second highest score is Green, and your lowest score is Blue. Your first response to conflict or opposition is most apt to be some form of challenge, some kind of "fighting off" behavior. You probably would experience the other person as being wrong and certainly not entitled to make you give up what you want to do. You will tend to experience your behavior as simply rising to the challenge that is being offered. And you will continue to feel this way until it dawns on you that trying to "fight off" the conflict is not going to make it go away.

At this point, you will probably try to protect your autonomy by backing off, defending yourself against any further intrusion and preserving whatever integrity you have left. You will tend to experience your behavior as trying to escape from the opposition. If this doesn't work, your last stand behavior will be to give in and, if your scores on the Blue are ten or lower, you will tend to feel totally defeated.

5. Your highest score is Green, your second highest score is Blue, and your lowest score is Red. Your first response to conflict and opposition is most likely to be one of becoming quite cautious. You will tend to pull back and examine your position, analyze what the conflict is all about, weigh events in terms of any possible violation of your principles, decide what is fair and then deal with the conflict on a logical basis. You will tend to experience your behavior as simply being prudent. And you will continue to feel this way until it dawns on you that this logical approach is not going to make the conflict go away.

At this point, you are most apt to go out of your way to be accommodating to the other person. You will tend to experience your behavior as giving in and letting the opposition have its way. If this doesn't work, your last stand behavior will be to finally fight for your rights and, if your scores are ten or lower on the Red, you will tend to experience your behavior as having to fight for your life, sometimes in very explosive ways.

6. Your highest score is Green, your second highest score is Red, and your lowest score is Blue. Your first response to conflict and opposition is most likely to be one of becoming quite cautious. You will tend to pull back and examine your position, analyze what the conflict is all about, weigh events in terms of any possible violation of your principles, decide what is fair and then deal with the conflict on a logical basis. You will tend to experience your behavior as simply being prudent. And you will continue to feel this way until it dawns on you that this logical approach is not going to make the conflict go away.

At this point, you will have come to the conclusion that the battle must be joined and you will tend to experience your behavior as having to fight off the opposition. If this doesn't work, your last stand behavior will be to give in and, if your scores on the Blue are ten or lower, you will tend to feel totally defeated.

If your highest score in columns four, five and six is at least seven points higher than the other two, and those two are six or less points apart, one of the following three descriptions will apply to you.

7. Your highest score is Blue, and your other two scores are within six points of each other. Your first response to conflict or opposition is most likely to be disbelief that conflict exists. You may feel that everything will be all right, that there is some simple misunderstanding that can be cleared up. You probably go a bit out of your way to be nice because, after all, if you're nice enough, the conflict will fade away. You will tend to experience your behavior as simply being accommodating to the needs of others. And you will continue to feel this way until it dawns on you that the conflict or opposition has not disappeared at all.

When this happens, you will fall back on logically based and assertive strategies to preserve your sense of self-worth in an attempt to stave off complete defeat.

8. Your highest score is Red, and your other two scores are within six points of each other. Your first response to conflict or opposition is most apt to be some form of challenge, some kind of "fighting off" behavior. You probably would experience the other person as being wrong and certainly not entitled to make you give up what you want to do. You will tend to experience your behavior as simply rising to the challenge that is being offered. And you will continue to feel this way until it dawns on you that trying to "fight off" the conflict is not going to make it go away.

When that happens, you will either give in for the moment or break off contact, whichever you see as most to your advantage.

9. Your highest score is Green, and your other two scores are within six points of each other. Your first response to conflict and opposition is most likely to be one of becoming quite cautious. You will tend to pull back and examine your position, analyze what the conflict is all about, weigh events in terms of any possible violation of your principles, decide what is fair and then deal with the conflict on a logical basis. You will tend to experience your behavior as simply being prudent. And you will continue to feel this way until it dawns on you that this logical approach is not going to make the conflict go away.

At this point, you will do one of two things. If the issue is important enough to you, you will fight for what you want. If the issue is not important to you, you will give in.

If your two highest scores in columns four, five and six are within six points of each other, and your third score is at least seven points lower than the lowest of those two scores, one of the following three descriptions will apply to you.

10. Your two highest scores are Blue and Red. Your first response to conflict and opposition is most likely one of pressing fairly assertively for the maintenance of harmony. You will probably feel that there has been some sort of misunderstanding and that if you can simply stand up for what it is you want, peace will be quickly restored. You probably experience your behavior as being both accommodating and assertive. If these efforts fail, however, you will finally withdraw from the situation.

11. Your two highest scores are Blue and Green. Your first response to conflict and opposition is most likely one of attempting to maintain harmony, while at the same time keeping a careful eye on the personal costs of doing so. You will probably feel that there has been some sort of logical misunderstanding, and that if you can simply get things clarified, peace will be quickly restored. If these efforts fail, you will finally fight for your rights, but only as a last resort and possibly explosively.

12. Your two highest scores are Red and Green. Your first response to conflict is to develop a set of strategies for dealing with the situation. You probably would experience the other person as being wrong and certainly not logically entitled to make you give up what you want to do. You will use your head to figure out how to get what you want. If this doesn't work, you will finally give in and surrender.

If all three of your scores in columns four, five and six are between 22 and 44, the following description will apply to you.

13. You are in the Hub. If your scores place you in the Hub in the face of conflict or opposition, you will shift from Blue to Red to Green. Since your scores are so close together, they may not indicate which set of behaviors you will choose first, which second, and which third. Your first response, however, will probably involve an attempt to make the conflict go away, your second a defense of your integrity and your third a last stand. *You* may know or begin to figure out which response you choose in different situations, but your scores give little indication of what that choice will be—it will depend on the circumstances.

Your Behavior in the Face of Conflict or Opposition

Now that you have a better understanding of what Relationship Awareness Theory has to say about the nature of conflict or opposition, please go back to the beginning of this chapter, where you were asked to describe a difficult or puzzling relationship. Reread your comments there, then answer the following question:

> In what ways does the concept of real conflict help you to understand the difficult relationship you described at the beginning of this chapter? In answering this question, be particularly aware of the ways your behavior changes in the face of continuing conflict or opposition.

The more you can understand the sequence you go through in using your strengths in the face of conflict or opposition, the more you will understand what is happening in those relationships or situations. You can be more accurate in understanding that sequence if you can identify the conditions under which you shift from one to the other. If one of the descriptions numbered one through six above described your behavior in the face of conflict, please indicate what needs to happen to move you from your first to your second level of response and then from your second to your third level of response.

Conditions under which I shift from my first level
of response to my second level of response:

_____
_____
_____
_____

Conditions under which I shift from my second
level of response to my third level of response:

_____
_____
_____
_____

If one of the descriptions numbered seven, eight, or nine described your behavior in the face of conflict or opposition, please identify below the conditions which cause you to shift from your first to your second two responses.

Conditions under which I shift from my first to my
second two responses:

_____
_____
_____
_____

Chapter Four

If one of the descriptions numbered ten, eleven, or twelve described your behavior in the face of conflict or opposition, please identify below the conditions which cause you to shift to your last ditch response.

    Conditions under which I shift from my first to my last ditch response:

_____
_____
_____
_____

For those of you who are in the hub in the face of conflict or opposition, you may wish to identify those kinds of situations, relationships or issues that lead you to choose a Blue response, a Red response, and a Green response.

    Conditions under which I tend to choose a Blue response to conflict:

_____
_____
_____
_____

Conditions under which I tend to choose a Red
response to conflict:

_____

_____

_____

_____

Conditions under which I tend to choose a Green
response to conflict:

_____

_____

_____

_____

Conclusion

Conflict is often a part of interpersonal relations. However, if you are aware of the gratifications you are seeking and know the gratifications being sought by the other person, you may assess whether a conflict is unwarranted or real. If it is unwarranted, you may devise ways of achieving a mutually gratifying, win-win relationship. If the conflict is real, you may attempt to change or limit that relationship or decide to terminate the relationship entirely. Whatever you decide to do can be done with insight and without violating your integrity or the integrity of the other person.

Chapter Four

Examples

Pages 35 & 36. Someone who is Red when things are going well and whose first response to conflict is Green might answer these statements as follows:

> 1. First, describe the nature of this difficult or puzzling relationship when things are going well for you. In general, what is going on in that relationship that makes it so difficult?
>
> *I feel very competitive in this relationship. I feel that Paul is always trying to "one up me."*
>
> 2. What specifically is it that the other person does to give you a problem or cause you difficulties?
>
> *He frequently disagrees with me in meetings and sometimes to others compares my work with his (to his advantage).*
>
> 3. When that happens, what is the first thing you usually do? How do you usually react when you experience this particular kind of difficulty with that person?
>
> *I guess I push back. I stand up for myself and let him know where I am coming from.*
>
> 4. Once you have done that, how does the other person usually respond?
>
> *He usually makes light of my response, says that I am taking things too personally (which is exactly how he intended them).*
>
> 5. Once the other person has responded in this way, what do you do? Do you continue with the behavior described in number three above, or does your behavior tend to change? If so, how does it change?

> *I really back off from him. I become very distant and, if I can, find some way of getting physically away from him.*

Page 50. This same person might answer these questions as follows:

> In what ways does the concept of real conflict help you to understand the difficult relationship you described at the beginning of this chapter? In answering this question, be particularly aware of the ways your behavior changes in the face of continuing conflict or opposition.
>
> *Paul and I are both Red when things are going well. When he challenges me and then makes light of my response, he really gives me no way to compete, so I just turn Green and try to get away from that situation. This always seems to work for me and I have never had the experience of having to drop back to Red (my next response) or Blue (my last resort response) with Paul.*

Page 51. This same person might complete these statements as follows:

> Conditions under which I shift from my first level of response to my second level of response.
>
> *When my Green is unable to get me out of that situation or I am unable to figure out what to do, I shift to Red and meet the challenge head-on.*
>
> Conditions under which I shift from my second level of response to my third level of response.
>
> *I will go Blue as a last resort only when I am unable to both think or fight my way out and only in a relationship to which I am highly committed. If this is the case I will finally—and with a sense of total defeat—give in.*

Chapter Five

Understanding Borrowed and "Mask" Relating Styles

At the conclusion of a seminar I conducted a few years ago on Relationship Awareness Theory, the participants were in the process of completing an evaluation of that experience. The last person by a wide margin to finish was a woman who had scored quite high on the Blue scale when things were going well. Several minutes after everyone finished their evaluations, she was still writing. Two or three participants who were waiting around for her to finish began to make joking comments about her being a Green instead of a Blue. Finally, having completed her evaluation and handed it to me, she said to her friends, "No, I don't think you are right about my being a Green. It seemed to me that the most helpful thing I could do in this situation would be to provide as much accurate information as I could about my responses to the seminar."

Most of the time, Blues are nurturant, Reds are assertive, Greens are analytical, and Hubs are flexible. But what about situations in which people are acting in ways that are not apparently consistent with their typical behavior? Here we had an individual with very high Blue scores acting in a way that at the moment would lead us to describe her as a Green. What's going on?

In the first two chapters we looked at the idea of needing to be aware not just of behavior but of the motivation that lies behind that behavior as well. At this point we need to look more carefully at that idea. Merely to observe behavior without being aware of the motivation associated with that behavior can lead us to make some very wrong assumptions about what another person is all about (and thus increase the chances of misunderstanding or unwarranted conflict). What is going on when you behave in ways that are quite different from your primary orientation as described on the **Strength Deployment Inventory**?

What Brings out the Blue, Red, Green and Hub in You?

I am certain that you can think of numerous situations in which you behaved like a Blue, a Red, a Green or a Hub, regardless of your primary orientation. Each of us, it would seem, can respond to various situations in a wide variety of ways.

Chapter Five

To help you get a sense of that for yourself, please complete the following statements, which will ask you to identify what brings out the Blue, Red, Green or Hub in you.

I am most apt to want to be helpful to other people when

_____

A recent example of when I did this would be

_____

I am most apt to want to take over leadership and direct others in what to do when

_____

A recent example of when I did this would be

_____

I am most apt to want to be self-dependent and rely mainly on myself when

_____

A recent example of when I did this would be

_____

I am most apt to want to be flexible and to keep my options open when

_____

A recent example of when I did this would be

_____

If you are a Blue, you probably answered the first statement with something like "Most of the time!" But I would guess that you found plenty of cases in which you behaved as a Red, a Green or a Hub. Now think back to those situations in which you acted in ways that would not be typical of your primary motivation. Ask yourself, "What was going on in those situations? Why was I behaving in that way?" and, most importantly, "What was the emotional satisfaction I was getting out of that behavior?"

If you are like most people, at least part of the time you were experiencing the rewards associated with that particular orientation. Simply because an individual is low, say, on the Red scale when things are going well does not mean that this individual never wants to be in charge. Under certain circumstances this individual can take charge and will feel good about himself or herself for providing leadership and direction. No matter what your score is on the Red scale, you have certainly had the experience at least occasionally of running the show, and it felt good, didn't it?

Although someone with a low score on a given scale will behave in ways associated with that scale less frequently than someone with higher scores on that scale, we all have increased our sense of self-worth by, at times, being helpful, directive, analytical, or flexible.

But you may also have thought about times when you were behaving in ways that were different from your primary orientation yet you were still operating out of the basic motivation associated with that orientation. In these cases you were using what Relationship Awareness Theory calls a Borrowed Relating Style.

Borrowed Relating Styles

A Borrowed Relating Style involves using behavior from another orientation as a tool in the pursuit of an individual's primary motivation. For a person with a high score on the Blue scale, disciplining a child in order to help him or her is a Borrowed Relating Style. Exercising discipline per se may do nothing for a person's sense of self-worth, but helping the child may do a great deal to help that person feel good about himself or herself. In a Borrowed Relating Style your behavior has changed but not your underlying purpose.

A school teacher's basic motivational pattern is Blue, but he is quite directive in the classroom and spends hours analyzing the needs of individual children. When asked why he behaves in ways that are both so assertive and so analytical, he answers that these behaviors serve to make him more genuinely helpful to his students.

A very assertive business person may appear to be the soul of consideration in relation to his employees, not out of any need to be nurturant, but out of a desire to win and hold their loyalty.

A lead engineer may be very directive with her people, not out of any need to be in charge, but out of a desire to do the project exactly as specified.

A team player can be rigid and inflexible if she sees that behavior as contributing to group cohesion.

The essential point in understanding the idea of a Borrowed Relating Style is that you may at times borrow behavior from other orientations if that behavior will help you toward the accomplishment of your primary orientation.

In the following four quotations each individual is describing behavior associated with all four of the basic orientations identified by Relationship Awareness Theory but is at the same time operating out of only one of those orientations. Circle the orientation out of which each of these four individuals is most likely operating.

"I'm determined that we will come out on top in this matter even if it means we have to be very patient with some of our distributors and show them the logic of the changes we require. We will need to be flexible in how we handle them but we must not let this cause us to slacken our resolve to win."

This person is most likely a

Blue	Red	Green	Hub

"The only way we can keep our options open so that we can move in whatever way is best at the moment is for all of us to continue to resist with all our will and to help each other in maintaining that resistance against any efforts to make us choose sides. We must fight side by side on this or end up with a divided house."

This person is most likely a

| Blue | Red | Green | Hub |

"If we are going to maintain our distance in this relationship we must be single-minded in our purpose and not be distracted from ever reaching our goal. At the same time we must be always alert to any new information and always willing to be as helpful as possible by letting people know exactly where we stand."

This person is most likely a

| Blue | Red | Green | Hub |

"I've found the most helpful thing I can do about his drinking is to be absolutely iron-willed in saying 'No' to him, hanging on to my position no matter what sad story he gives me, and being flexible enough to counter each new strategy he tries."

This person is most likely a

| Blue | Red | Green | Hub |

In the first example the person seems to be operating out of a Red motivation but is borrowing behavior from the other three orientations to achieve his or her objectives of winning.

In the second example the person seems to be operating out of a Hub motivation but is borrowing behavior from the other three orientations to achieve his or her objectives of maintaining flexibility and group cohesion.

In the third example the person seems to be operating out of a Green motivation but is borrowing behavior from the other three orientations to achieve his or her objectives of self-dependence and self-reliance.

In the fourth example the person seems to be operating out of a Blue motivation but is borrowing behavior from the other three orientations to achieve his or her objectives of being helpful.

Using Borrowed Relating Styles

You might find the following three suggestions useful in helping you use your own Borrowed Relating Styles more effectively.

> First, be aware of the way you tend to overdo your strengths. You may well find that in those situations you would be better advised to borrow a relating style from another orientation rather than to push on with your own valued relating style.
>
> Second, give yourself permission to behave in ways that are not consistent with your primary orientation. If you are high on the Assertive-Directing scale, for instance, be aware that you do not always have to be Red, that it is sometimes all right to be nurturant, analytical, or flexible.
>
> Third, consciously set about to improve your skills in using the behaviors associated with orientations other than your own. Carefully observe the behavior of others whose valued relating styles are different from your own. You can incorporate into your own behavior the best of all four orientations.

In understanding your own behavior, be aware of the fact that you behave in a variety of ways, as a way of furthering your primary orientation. And in understanding the behavior of others, be very careful in drawing conclusions about a person's motivation from a single piece of behavior.

As is always the case with Relationship Awareness Theory, look at behavior as a vehicle that moves someone toward the accomplishment of the objective of feeling worthwhile about himself or herself as a person. Most of the time we accomplish this by using the behavior associated with our primary orientation. But we can also accomplish this from time to time by borrowing behavior from other orientations.

"Mask" Relating Styles

But what about those times when you find yourself using behavior from another orientation in ways that do not enhance your feelings of self-worth?

> *An employee whose feelings of personal worth arise from being of genuine help to other people is thrust into a situation in which, to be successful, she must be competitive and demonstrate the kind of leadership that puts task accomplishment ahead of people's feelings.*

This is not to say that this person cannot master these new behaviors. Organizations sometimes force people to behave in ways that violate their personal integrity. When you use a relating style from another orientation, either through force or because you feel it is expected of you, you have adopted what Relationship Awareness Theory calls a "Mask" Relating Style.

A "Mask" Relating Style is a style of relating that a person learns to put on like a mask because it is expected, required, or needed, perhaps as the only means of survival.

> *An Assertive-Directing sales person, in order to move up the corporate ladder, is forced to spend two years teaching younger men and women to be sales people.*

> *An Analytic-Autonomizing engineer is put in charge of a project group and told to deliver the product by a certain deadline no matter what.*

> *An Altruistic-Nurturing nurse is forced to become head of the Nursing Department; or a Flexible-Cohering manager is forced to do a routine job in exactly the same way day after day.*

From time to time you have been forced to behave in ways that were not consistent with your primary orientation. Hopefully you were able to navigate your way through these episodes in ways that did little or no damage to your self-esteem. But if, in any significant way, you have found yourself forced to behave in these ways, you know the emotional costs involved. In the long term, using a "Mask" Relating Style diminishes a person's feeling of self-worth and lowers that person's sense of self-esteem.

Think of a time in your life in which you were expected or required or even forced to behave in ways that were not compatible with your primary orientation, then provide the information requested below.

First, describe in general the situation or relationship you found yourself in when you were forced to use a "Mask" Relating Style.

_____

_____

Next, describe specifically the ways you were expected or forced to behave. In what ways did that "Mask" Relating Style differ from your Valued Relating Style?

_____

_____

Finally, describe how you felt about yourself as a person during that period in which you were using that "Mask" Relating Style.

_____

_____

Again, the point here is not that we can't be successful using a "Mask" Relating Style. The point is instead the emotional cost of doing so.

A Classic Example

The following is a classic example of an experience Dr. Porter had with a "Mask" Relating Style. He provided this example in numerous seminars and consultations, and it has been frequently repeated by many of us in the field in our own workshops. It is, however, such a dramatic example of the way a "Mask" Relating Style can work that it deserves repeating here one more time.

On one occasion Dr. Porter had in one of his seminars a woman whose scores on the Strength Deployment Inventory when things were going well were high and relatively equal on the Red and Green scales and correspondingly low on the Blue; in other words, as a person with a Judicious-Competing orientation, she felt best about herself when she could use her head to accomplish her objectives.

This woman described herself as having been very successful at her first job, which was as a kindergarten teacher. She was apparently well-liked by the parents and the school's administrators and was loved by the children. No one could figure out, however, why, during her last two years in that job, she cried every day on her way to work.

As a kindergarten teacher, this woman found herself in a position in which nurturant behavior was expected and even required. She apparently could do that behavior quite skillfully, but it was a behavior that was barren for her in providing her with any sense of self-worth.

After she told her story, Dr. Porter asked her if there had been anything in that job that did make her feel good about herself as a person. After thinking for a moment, she replied, "Yes, I did feel good about myself when I encountered a child who was having trouble learning certain material, for then I had to figure out how to get that kid to do what I wanted him or her to do."

Only when she was able to operate in accordance with her Red/Green orientation, that is, only while she was using her head to win, did she feel worthwhile as a person.

Conclusion

An important issue here is the extent to which a person is aware of the fact that he or she is using a "Mask" Relating Style. All too often, you may know that something is wrong but not realize the true nature of the problem. In trying to figure out why she cried on the way to work each morning, the kindergarten teacher at first said that, of course, her job could not have been the problem since she was so good at it.

The Peter Principle states that in a hierarchical organization people

Laurence J. Peter and Raymond Hull, *The Peter Principle* (William Morrow and Company: New York, 1969).

tend to rise to their level of incompetence. One way of understanding this idea is to look at the ways so many people in so many organizations are forced to put on a "Mask" Relating Style as they move up the hierarchy. The tragedy is that far too often the individual involved is not aware of what is happening.

Relationship Awareness Theory can help you understand those periods in your life when, perhaps only half-consciously, you found yourself being forced to act in ways that did not enhance your self-esteem. Relationship Awareness Theory can also give you the understanding needed to avoid or change situations or relationships in the present and in the future that do not help you feel good about yourself as a person.

Examples

Page 58. Someone with high scores on the Green scale might complete these statements as follows:

> I am most apt to want to be helpful to other people when
>
> *I know it's the right thing to do or when I can support the other person to do what he or she knows is right.*
>
> A recent example of when I did this would be
>
> *when I spent an hour last week just listening to Joan talk about her problems with her new job. I know she will do the right thing but that she just needs some time to work out her ideas.*
>
> I am most apt to want to take over leadership and direct others in what to do when
>
> *no one else seems willing to take charge and the issue is one I believe in very much, one that I know I'm right about.*

A recent example of when I did this would be

the leading role I took on that local environmental task force last year. Something had to be done about those problems and—well, it just seemed the right thing to do.

I am most apt to want to be self-dependent and rely mainly on myself

most of the time, particularly when I sense that someone is trying to rush me into making a decision.

A recent example of when I did this would be

that workshop evaluation I had to complete last week. I told them that I would decide if the ideas were worthwhile after I have had a chance to try them out for a couple of weeks.

I am most apt to want to be flexible and to keep my options open when

I find myself facing an issue I don't know much about but which others seem invested in. If the issue is not very important to me I'm usually willing to be flexible and go with what the majority wants to do.

A recent example of when I did this would be

the decision the safety committee made last week— I don't work in that area, so it didn't much matter to me how they want to set things up.

Chapter Five

Page 64. Someone with high scores on the Blue scale might respond to these statements as follows:

> First, describe in general the situation or relationship you found yourself in when you were forced to used a "Mask" Relating Style.
>
> *I think the best example of this was the "promotion" I got at AMI about six months before I left that company. Up until that time I had been in a staff position, one in which I was able to be helpful to a number of people in the company.*
>
> Next, describe specifically the ways you were expected or forced to behave. In what ways did that "Mask" Relating Style differ from your Valued Relating Style?
>
> *I guess because of my success, I was promoted to head of Employee Development just before the big merger with SDS Industries. I had to bring our two departments together, reduce staff by 30%, then take the lead in developing a whole new technical training program. And because of budget problems I was told that we would do no additional human relations training for at least the next two years.*
>
> Finally, describe how you felt about yourself as a person during that period in which you were using that "Mask" Relating Style.
>
> *I just hated it. I didn't like having to fire people, and I certainly wasn't much interested in all that technical training. I was able to do those things, but I wasn't very happy at it. I guess what finally made me begin to look for another job, however, was the lack of emphasis the company was putting on human relations training. The new, reorganized company just didn't seem to care about its people anymore.*

Chapter Six

Understanding Others

Up to now, you have been learning about yourself in light of Relationship Awareness Theory and about the ways it applies to you. Hopefully you have found these ideas of value as you have become more aware of yourself in relation to others. As you have been reading these chapters, however, you have probably begun to apply Relationship Awareness Theory to your understanding of other people as well. It is now time to look more closely at what these ideas can tell us about others.

Our reasons for wanting to understand others will, of course, vary and may well reflect our own primary orientation on the **Strength Deployment Inventory**. Blues will want to understand others so that they can help them. Reds will want to understand others so that they can more effectively direct them toward task accomplishment. Greens will want to understand others as a way of assuring their own autonomy. Hubs will want to understand others so as to know in what ways they need to be flexible and adaptable. If we can learn to understand others better, we will be in a better position to deploy our own valued relating style. If we can learn to interact with others in ways that can help make both ourselves and the other person feel worthwhile as people, we will have taken an important step toward creating win-win relationships and avoiding unwarranted conflict.

Understanding Another's Orientation

There are a number of ways to understand another person's interpersonal orientation. First, of course, although you cannot very likely give the **Strength Deployment Inventory** to everyone you know, you might nevertheless consider giving the questionnaire to a few of the important people in your life. A spouse, a friend, a teen-age child, or a trusted colleague might be willing to complete the questionnaire and provide you with his or her scores. If you do that, however, you probably should be prepared to provide that person with some information about Relationship Awareness Theory. Since that person has shared his or her scores with you, you might also be prepared to do the same with your own scores. Perhaps it would be appropriate to provide that person with their own copy of this book in preparation for the discussion about these ideas and your relationship with that individual that will almost certainly result from a sharing of scores.

> A parallel questionnaire to the **Strength Deployment Inventory** has been developed called the **Personal Values Inventory** for use with people of relatively limited vocabularies. This instrument would certainly be appropriate for most teen-agers.

Chapter Six

A companion questionnaire to the **Personal Values Inventory**, called the "Mirror Edition," is also available. All of these instruments can be obtained from Personal Strengths Publishing, Inc., P. O. Box 397, Pacific Palisades, California 90272, (310) 454-5915.

A second way of estimating a person's interpersonal orientation would be to complete the "Feedback Edition" of the **Strength Deployment Inventory** about that individual. Although this questionnaire is primarily intended to be completed by someone else—a friend, spouse, boss, subordinate, or peer—to show how they experience your behavior, there is no reason why you couldn't complete it about another person according to the way you experience that person in interaction with you, which can help you clarify your perception of that individual in terms of Relationship Awareness Theory. This could be done, of course, without involving the other person and thus might be appropriate in helping you understand a difficult or troubled relationship.

A third way of gaining a sense of where another person is coming from is simply to pay attention to that person in terms of what you have already learned about Relationship Awareness Theory. You should now be clear about what these ideas are all about and should be ready to apply them to your understanding of others.

To demonstrate this I would like you to complete the following two charts. The first provides a list of some of the issues that are of typical concern to Blues, Reds, Greens, and Hubs, while the second identifies some of the typical ways people of different orientations behave. In each case, circle the letter ("B" for Blues, "R" for Reds, and so forth) that identifies the orientation you associate with those issues and behaviors. Remember, of course, that in actual practice you may be looking at a borrowed or a masked relating style and thus come to an incorrect conclusion about that individual. The more information you have about a person's behavior under a variety of circumstances, the better chance you will have of describing that person's orientation correctly.

Understanding Others

Issues of Typical Concern to People

1. B R G H	Taking action now	11. B R G H	Accuracy
2. B R G H	Conserving resources	12. B R G H	Taking risks
3. B R G H	Maintaining harmony	13. B R G H	Precision
4. B R G H	Doing whatever the situation requires	14. B R G H	Learning about the available options
5. B R G H	Welfare of others	15. B R G H	Challenges
6. B R G H	Creating order	16. B R G H	Competing
7. B R G H	Getting things done	17. B R G H	Being flexible
8. B R G H	How people feel	18. B R G H	Being fair
9. B R G H	Being persuasive	19. B R G H	Group agreement
10. B R G H	Being careful	20. B R G H	Being strong

Typical Ways of Behaving

1. B R G H	Cautious	11. B R G H	Trusts others
2. B R G H	Finds opportunities	12. B R G H	Highly flexible
3. B R G H	Giving	13. B R G H	Reserves judgment
4. B R G H	Takes leadership	14. B R G H	Orderly
5. B R G H	Sets goals	15. B R G H	Altruistic
6. B R G H	Identifies with group	16. B R G H	Logical
7. B R G H	Persuades others	17. B R G H	Idealistic
8. B R G H	Helps others	18. B R G H	Quick to act
9. B R G H	Practical	19. B R G H	Analytical
10. B R G H	Generates alternatives	20. B R G H	Thorough

One set of answers to these items is given at the end of the chapter. Although you and I may differ on our interpretation of a few of these, I think you will have found that you can now assess another person's orientation with some degree of confidence. Once you have understood where that other person is coming from, you can get on his or her wavelength, as it were, and begin to build a more consistent win-win relationship with that individual.

In beginning to attend more closely to the behavior of others, remember our discussion in Chapters One and Two about the relationship between behavior and motivation. Don't stop at identifying someone as, for example, a Red, and then assume that that person will always act in an Assertive-Directing manner. Remember to look behind that behavior to understand the motive, sources of satisfaction, and personal gratification for which that behavior is only a vehicle. Also be aware of the possibility of borrowed or mask relating styles. If you do this, you will have begun to understand other people, for you have begun to understand what makes them feel worthwhile about themselves as human beings.

Building More Productive Relationships

To improve our relationships with others, we need first of all to be more aware of what we find attractive about each orientation, more sensitive to the kinds of difficulties we tend to have with each orientation, and to develop some specific ideas as to what we might do to reduce those difficulties. To accomplish that, please provide the following information.

What I like about

Blue is
_____
_____

Red is
_____
_____

Greens is

_____

_____

Hubs is

_____

_____

The difficulties I tend to have with

Blues are

_____

_____

Reds are

_____

_____

Chapter Six

Greens are

_____

_____

Hubs are

_____

_____

Now, keeping in mind your own orientation on the **Strength Deployment Inventory**, begin identifying some specific things *you* could begin doing to reduce some of the difficulties you tend to have with each of these four interpersonal orientations.

I could improve my relationships with

Blues by

_____

_____

Reds by

_____

_____

Greens by
_____
_____

Hubs by
_____
_____

Now that you know more about yourself in relationship with Blues, Reds, Greens and Hubs and have identified some specific things you could begin doing to improve your interactions with each of those orientations, you may find it helpful to identify what others find rewarding.

Listed below are twelve rewards. Next to each please identify which orientation would be most likely to feel rewarded. One set of responses is again provided at the end of this chapter.

Who would be most likely to feel rewarded by being provided with

1. B R G H	Accurate information		7. B R G H	A chance to benefit others
2. B R G H	A chance to seize opportunity		8. B R G H	A chance to provide support
3. B R G H	A chance to help others who need help		9. B R G H	Money as a way of keeping score
4. B R G H	A chance to do meaningful work alone		10. B R G H	Contribution to group effort
5. B R G H	A chance to try new or varied tasks		11. B R G H	Time to explore options
6. B R G H	Time for analysis		12. B R G H	Leadership and authority

The often-asked question "How do I motivate people?" is not a very good one. It is impossible to motivate anyone other than ourselves. We can provide others with incentives and rewards, but people provide their own motivation. The challenge is to tap the motivation that lies within a person, a motivation that already exists.

Once you understand another person's orientation in terms of Relationship Awareness Theory, a better question to ask is "What can I do to provide opportunities for the other person to behave in ways that would enhance his or her feelings of self-worth?" If we can provide an environment that is rich in the things people of a particular orientation find rewarding, motivation will take care of itself. Consider the following case study.

> *The largely Assertive-Directing management team of a large urban hospital became convinced of the need to cut back significantly on expenses. One alternative, of course, was to simply mandate the new spending guidelines, but the team had experienced very little success with this approach in the past. After being trained in Relationship Awareness Theory, however, the management team took a quite different approach.*
>
> *Correctly assuming that the nursing staff was largely Blue, they approached them by saying "We are going to continue to provide the best possible health care, but to be able to do that we must cut down on unnecessary expenses. You are the ones who can help us do that. What do you suggest we do?"*
>
> *Correctly assuming that most of the technical and laboratory staff was largely Green, the management team approached them by saying "We will continue to provide detailed, in-depth analysis when needed, but to do that we must cut down on unnecessary and wasteful lab work. You are the ones who have that information. What should we do?"*
>
> *The responses from both groups far exceeded expectations, and the management team was able to cut expenses appropriately and successfully.*

A win-win relationship is one in which both parties are able to interact in their valued relating style. Understanding the orientation of the other person, while keeping in mind your own orientation,

Understanding Others

can significantly increase the likelihood that any single interpersonal interaction can be mutually rewarding for everyone involved.

Understanding One Other Person

Ultimately, Relationship Awareness Theory will only be of value to you if it can help you more effectively manage your own relationships with other people. To help you begin doing that, I would like to take you through a series of activities that will focus on your relationship with one specific person in your life. That could be a person you value highly or someone with whom you have a difficult or puzzling relationship. You might want to select someone who would be willing to sit down with you later to go over your responses, although that is not essential.

The first step in this process would be to identify the interpersonal orientation of the other person. On the basis of your current understanding of Relationship Awareness Theory you may be able to make that assessment right now. If not, or if you would like to confirm your assessment of that individual, please look over the following two lists (they are ones you have worked with earlier in this chapter) and circle the issues or behaviors you associate with that individual.

> Because your responses in this section will be unique to you and specific to the relationship you are analyzing, completed examples for this section have not been given at the end of this chapter.

Issues of Typical Concern to this Person

1. Taking action now	8. How people feel	15. Challenges
2. Conserving resources	9. Being persuasive	16. Competing
3. Maintaining harmony	10. Being careful	17. Being flexible
4. Doing whatever the situation requires	11. Accuracy	18. Being fair
5. Welfare of others	12. Taking risks	19. Group agreement
6. Creating order	13. Precision	20. Being strong
7. Getting things done	14. Learning about available options	

Typical Ways this Person Behaves

1. Cautious	8. Helps others	15. Altruistic
2. Finds opportunities	9. Practical	16. Logical
3. Giving	10. Generates alternatives	17. Idealistic
4. Takes leadership	11. Trusts others	18. Quick to act
5. Sets goals	12. Highly flexible	19. Analytical
6. Identifies with group	13. Reserves judgement	20. Thorough
7. Persuades others	14. Orderly	

If you are still unsure of this person's orientation, you may want to follow an old rule that says "When in doubt, guess Hub." If you see this person behaving sometimes as a Blue, sometimes as a Red, and sometimes as a Green, that individual may well be operating out of the Hub.

On the basis of this analysis, circle the orientation or blend of orientations which you feel most accurately describes this person.

Blue
Altruistic-
Nurturing

Red
Assertive-
Directing

Green
Analytic-
Autonomizing

Hub
Flexible-Cohering

Blue/Green
Cautious-
Supporting

Red/Blue
Assertive-
Nurturing

Red/Green
Judicious-
Competing

Now complete the following statement:

This individual seems to feel best about himself or herself when he or she can _____

_____

Next, from the following list of characteristic strengths, circle what you see as this individual's three most characteristic strengths.

Blue	Red	Green	Hub
Trusting	Self-Confident	Cautious	Flexible
Optimistic	Enterprising	Practical	Open to change
Loyal	Ambitious	Economical	Socializer
Idealistic	Organizer	Reserved	Experimenter
Helpful	Persuasive	Methodical	Curious
Modest	Forceful	Analytic	Adaptable
Devoted	Quick to act	Principled	Tolerant
Caring	Imaginative	Orderly	Open to Compromise
Supportive	Competitive	Fair	Looks for Options
Accepting	Proud	Persevering	Socially sensitive
Polite	Bold	Conserving	Team player
Undemanding	Risk-taking	Thorough	Mediator

Now list these strengths in order in the space provided.

This individual's three most characteristic strengths are:

1. Most characteristic strength:
_____

2. Second most characteristic strength:
_____

3. Third most characteristic strength:
_____

In Chapter Two you identified your six most characteristic strengths. Write the first three of those strengths in the spaces provided below.

My most characteristic strengths are:

1. Most characteristic strength:
_____

2. Next most characteristic strength:
_____

3. Third most characteristic strength:
_____

On the basis of this analysis, describe below the nature of your relationship with this person when the relationship seems to be working, that is, when you are feeling good about yourself as a person in that relationship and when the other person seems to be feeling good about himself or herself as well.

When this relationship is working, we are:

_____
_____
_____

Next, from the following list, circle the three strengths that you see this person most likely to overdo.

Blue	Red	Green	Hub
Trusting *Gullible*	Self-Confident *Arrogant*	Cautious *Suspicious*	Flexible *Inconsistent*
Optimistic *Impractical*	Enterprising *Opportunistic*	Practical *Unimaginative*	Open to change *Wishy-washy*
Loyal *Slavish*	Ambitious *Ruthless*	Economical *Stingy*	Socializer *Can't be alone*
Idealistic *Wishful*	Organizer *Controller*	Reserved *Cold*	Experimenter *Aimless*
Helpful *Self-denying*	Persuasive *Pressuring*	Methodical *Rigid*	Curious *Nosy*
Modest *Self-effacing*	Forceful *Dictatorial*	Analytic *Nit-picking*	Adaptable *Spineless*
Devoted *Self-sacrificing*	Quick to act *Rash*	Principled *Unbending*	Tolerant *Uncaring*
Caring *Smothering*	Imaginative *Dreamer*	Orderly *Compulsive*	Open to Compromise *No principles*
Supportive *Submissive*	Competitive *Combative*	Fair *Unfeeling*	Looks for Options *No focus*
Accepting *Passive*	Proud *Conceited*	Persevering *Stubborn*	Socially sensitive *Dependent*
Polite *Deferential*	Bold *Brash*	Conserving *Possessive*	Team player *Groupie*
Undemanding *Masochistic*	Risk-taking *Gambler*	Thorough *Obsessive*	Mediator *No convictions*

Chapter Six

Next, write those strengths in order in the space provided.

The strengths this individual is most likely to overdo are:

---

1. The first strength this person is most likely to overdo is being

   _____. When he or she overdoes this strength I tend to see him

   or her as _____.

2. The strength this person is next most likely to overdo is being

   _____. When he or she overdoes this strength I tend to

   see him or her as _____.

3. The strength this person is next most likely to overdo is

   being _____. When he or she overdoes this strength I tend to

   see him or her as _____.

In Chapter Three you identified the three strengths you were most likely to overdo. Please write those in the space provided below.

The strengths I am most likely to overdo are:

---

1. My most frequently overdone strength is _____.
The usual reaction that most people have to that overdone strength is
_____

2. My second most frequently overdone strength is _____.
The usual reaction that most people have to that overdone strength is
_____

3. My third most frequently overdone strength is _____.
The usual reaction that most people have to that overdone strength is
_____

On the basis of this analysis, describe as accurately as you can what is going on in your relationship with this individual when things are not working, when one or both of you does not seem to be feeling very good about yourselves.

When this relationship is not working, we are:

_____

_____

Finally, complete the following four statements.

1. Some of the things I could do to help keep this relationship working are

_____

2. Some of the things I could do to help keep this relationship from getting into trouble are

_____

3. Some of the things I would like from the other person to help make this relationship work are

_____

4. Some of the things I could do to help the other person keep this relationship working are

_____

Again, depending on the nature of your relationship with this individual, you might want to sit down with him or her and review your responses. If the other person has also taken the **Strength Deployment Inventory** and has also worked through this section of the book, that conversation could be very productive. But whether or not you have done that, you have begun to make Relationship Awareness Theory work for you in the way it is intended, and that is to have these ideas make a difference in the way you relate to the important people in your life.

Conclusion

Improving interpersonal relationships takes time, attention, and effort. And as so often in life, it is the little things that make a difference.

> *Consider, for example, a husband (Red) and wife (Hub) who had decided to buy a second car. Understanding his wife's needs to look at alternatives and options, the husband went out one Saturday afternoon by himself and identified six different cars that met the criteria he and his wife had agreed upon for the purchase. He then gave the list to his wife, indicating that any of the six cars would be fine with him. After spending a considerable amount of time looking over all six cars by herself, she finally chose one with which she was happy.*

In this example, the husband felt good about himself because he had been able to exercise initiative and direction toward getting a goal accomplished, while at the same time providing his wife with plenty of flexibility. Think how different this story would have been if the husband, as a Red might well have done, had simply gone out and selected the "best" car, then tried to convince his wife of the correctness of that single choice. Think how a Hub might respond when given no alternatives to consider. The difference between win-win and lose-lose relationships is often a matter of attention to such small details as this.

Examples

Page 71. Various interpretations of several of these issues and ways of behaving are possible, but one set of responses to these items that most people would agree with would be as follows:

Issues of Typical Concern to People

1. Red	Taking action now	11. Green	Accuracy
2. Green	Conserving resources	12. Red	Taking risks
3. Blue	Maintaining harmony	13. Green	Precision
4. Hub	Doing whatever the situation requires	14. Hub	Learning about available options
5. Blue	Welfare of others	15. Red	Challenges
6. Green	Creating order	16. Red	Competing
7. Red	Getting things done	17. Hub	Being flexible
8. Blue	How people feel	18. Green	Being fair
9. Red	Being persuasive	19. Hub	Group agreement
10. Green	Being careful	20. Red	Being strong

Typical Ways of Behaving

1. Green	Cautious	11. Blue	Trusts others
2. Red	Finds opportunities	12. Hub	Highly flexible
3. Blue	Giving	13. Green	Reserves judgment
4. Red	Takes leadership	14. Green	Orderly
5. Red	Sets goals	15. Blue	Altruistic
6. Hub	Identifies with group	16. Green	Logical
7. Red	Persuades others	17. Blue	Idealistic
8. Blue	Helps others	18. Red	Quick to act
9. Green	Practical	19. Green	Analytical
10. Hub	Generates alternatives	20. Green	Thorough

Chapter Six

Pages 72 & 73. A Hub might respond to these statements as follows:

What I like about

> Blues is
>
> *the way they are able to respond to the needs of others, particularly to the needs of groups, to help everyone feel involved and important.*
>
> Reds is
>
> *their ability to get the group organized to accomplish a task. They are often ready to move into action when, if they were not around, I would still be trying to figure out what to do.*
>
> Greens is
>
> *the balance they provide both the Blues and the Reds. They will go after the information Blues often ignore and help slow the Reds down from taking action too quickly.*
>
> Hubs is
>
> *their interest in variety. As a Hub, variety is very important to me, and other Hubs help provide me with new ideas, with new and different ways of looking at things.*

The difficulties I tend to have with

> Blues are
>
> *when they become too Blue, particularly when they become so smothering and "helpful" that no one in the group seems to have any space to work things out for themselves.*
>
> Reds are
>
> *when they move too quickly into action without considering all of the alternatives. There are times when a more considered approach is necessary.*

Understanding Others

> Greens are
>
> *when they will not move at all. This sounds like a contradiction to what I said about Reds, but sometimes Greens seem absolutely unable to move into action at all.*
>
> Hubs are
>
> *fairly infrequent— after all, I am one. But I guess sometimes even Hubs can delay too long in making a decision, and then I get impatient. But that doesn't happen very often.*

Page 74. This same person might continue on with these statements as follows:

I could improve my relationships with

> Blues by
>
> *by letting them be Blue and becoming more aware of my ability to balance them by being Red or Green as needed. When Blues are around I don't need to be Blue.*
>
> Reds by
>
> *being more willing to make a decision and take action sooner. As a Hub I do sometimes keep my options open far too long, and I know that this must be frustrating to Reds.*
>
> Greens by
>
> *setting clearer limits on the amount of information collection needed for a particular project. Sometimes I don't do this and Greens will then continue their research forever.*
>
> Hubs by
>
> *being aware of my own tendency to lose focus and wander too far afield and by being very careful that when I am working with other Hubs I do not reinforce this tendency.*

Chapter Six

Page 75. Again, although various intrepretations of these items is possible, the following answers should meet with general agreement.

Most likely to feel rewarded by being provided with:

1. Green	Accurate information	7. Blue	A chance to benefit others
2. Red	A chance to seize opportunity	8. Blue	A chance to provide support
3. Blue	A chance to help others who need help	9. Red	Money as a way of keeping score
4. Green	A chance to do meanfull work alone	10. Hub	Contribution to group effort
5. Hub	A chance try new or varied tasks	11. Hub	Time to explore options
6. Green	Time for analysis	12. Red	Leadership and authority

Chapter Seven

Understanding Work

The world of work involves people in interaction with each other, and consequently Relationship Awareness Theory can be of great value in understanding what goes on in the workplace. In the next chapter I'll suggest ways you might want to begin using these concepts to understand such specific work related issues as conflict management, time management, career development and sales training. The majority of this chapter will be devoted to an examination of three much broader issues —organizational cultures, team building, and management—and then will show how you can begin applying these concepts to your own job.

Understanding Organizational Cultures

A great deal of attention has been paid over the last several years to the idea of organizational cultures. Like a small country, every organization has its own culture—its own ways of doing things, its particular heroes, its own stories and rituals. Through understanding more about the culture of a particular organization, we can understand more about that organization's particular strengths and weaknesses, internal conflicts and pressures, and the day-to-day life of its members.

Perhaps the most useful of these attempts has been presented by Terrence Deal and Allan Kennedy in *Corporate Cultures: The Rites and Rituals of Corporate Life* (Addison-Wesley Publishing Company: Reading, Massachusetts, 1982).

One of the most powerful ways of understanding organizations is through the insights provided by Relationship Awareness Theory. Some organizational cultures are relatively simple to describe. Many social service agencies, for example, are Blue or Blue-Green, many sales organizations Red, many accounting firms Green, and many law firms Red-Green. To the extent that an organizational culture is characterized by a single orientation, many of the insights provided by Relationship Awareness Theory to individual behavior can be applied to the organization as well.

Take, for example, a School of Nursing in a major state university. As we might expect, all of the nurses who made up the teaching faculty were Blue. The head of the school, although somewhat higher on the Red scale than her faculty, was also Blue.

As part of a major reorganization of the university, this School of Nursing was fighting for its survival. It was about to be merged into a larger administrative unit and thus lose

> *its own budget, its own autonomy, its own curriculum—in short, its very existence. In the battles that preceded this merger, every time the head of the school went out into the university to oppose the reorganization she received clear messages from her faculty that this was not appropriate behavior, that it "was not nice to fight," and that the best thing the school could do would be to be patient and hope everything would work out all right.*
>
> *The nursing school was, of course, swallowed up in the reorganization and no longer exists today.*

Blues, whether individuals or organizations, are vulnerable to being taken advantage of by others. Like an individual high on the Blue scale, the School of Nursing in this example needed to borrow more successfully from the Red orientation in its fight for survival.

Most organizations, however, cannot be described this simply but can nevertheless be understood in terms of Relationship Awareness Theory. Instead of looking at the organization as if it were a single individual, look at what goes on in an organization as the result of the interaction of different orientations.

> *Take, for example, a major construction firm that worked primarily with the military. Most of the middle and senior managers, many of whom were retired military officers, scored quite high in the Red. Pressures for productivity in this highly competitive industry were intense, with constant demands by management to come in on each project ahead of schedule and under budget.*
>
> *First line supervisors in this organization, however, scored quite high on the Blue scale when things were going well but went Green when faced with conflict or opposition. One of those supervisors described his job as "protecting my people from the jerks in this organization." Although he actually used a somewhat stronger word than "jerks," it was clear he meant upper management.*
>
> *This organization has a long history of poor union-management relationships, frequent wildcat strikes, and lock-outs. Two years ago the organization filed for bankruptcy.*

Like individuals experiencing unwarranted conflict, the Red demands for productivity were met at the supervisory level by people who felt good about themselves when they could protect their subordinates from those pressures. And again, like individuals experiencing real conflict, when these supervisors could no longer protect their people and thus feel good about themselves, they retreated into the Green, either by becoming physically difficult to locate or demanding a literal and point by point enforcement of the union contract.

The purpose of creating an organization is to accomplish things together that cannot be accomplished alone. To the extent that people of the same orientation come together to accomplish the objectives characteristic of that orientation, the organization will have many of the same characteristics of individuals high on that orientation. To the extent that people of different orientations come together to accomplish different objectives, the potential for both unwarranted and real conflict exists. The same insights that Relationship Awareness Theory offers for the understanding of interpersonal relations can also be useful for understanding the larger, but nevertheless similar, dynamics of organizations.

Team Building

If the reason why people join and create organizations is to accomplish together things that they cannot accomplish alone, the actual work of those organizations is most often accomplished in groups. Group work is perhaps *the* central fact of organizational life, and the quality of the relationships in those groups invariably determines the level of success an organization will enjoy. Nowhere can the concepts of Relationship Awareness Theory be more helpful than in understanding how to establish and maintain effective, productive groups.

> *A small medical office had as a primary function scheduling and billing for a group of physicians. The office was operated by four people. In charge was an experienced registered nurse who scored about 65 on the Blue scale. The actual work of the office was performed by two young men, both of whom were hubs, and an older woman, whose score was about 70 on the Green scale. The two young men, of course, wanted to do everything as a team, which the older woman refused to do, preferring to work on her own, in her own way and at her own pace. The friction between the two Hubs on the one hand and the Green woman on the other had become intense and caused constant disruption of the work of the office.*

In attempting to resolve these conflicts, one, two, and sometimes all three of these individuals would descend on the Blue nurse, demanding that she resolve each issue in favor of one side or the other. As Blues so often are, however, she was very uncomfortable with conflict and therefore tended to avoid the demands of all three of her subordinates, hoping that time would restore the peace and tranquility with which she was more comfortable. This, however, only caused the conflict to increase, while at the same time undermining the relationship between the nurse and her subordinates.

After all four people had been trained in Relationship Awareness Theory, the Blue nurse became convinced that her avoidance of conflict was not helping at all, and that the most helpful thing she could do would be to settle these disputes firmly and fairly. Her three subordinates, however, became aware of how difficult this might be for her as a Blue and so came up with the idea that any major problem would be saved for a meeting of all four people to be held late every Friday afternoon. The nurse would then have the weekend to make up her mind and would be expected to announce her decision on Monday morning. Although making these decisions was difficult for her, she had been convinced that this would be the most helpful thing she could do, and the conflict and tension in the office gradually evaporated.

Several points about the use of Relationship Awareness Theory for team building can be made from this case study.

Do not underestimate the power of awareness. Perhaps the most useful contribution to group effectiveness that Relationship Awareness Theory can make is to help people become aware of and value the interpersonal orientation of another person, for it is this awareness that can reduce the frequency of unwarranted conflict.

Do not expect Relationship Awareness Theory to provide the answer. What Relationship Awareness Theory can provide is insight. Once individual group members have gained that insight, they are usually capable of solving their own problems.

Do not expect Hubs necessarily to be good team members. Hubs will be more *concerned* about the team and will often feel best about themselves when they are able to operate as part of an effective team but, as this case study demonstrates, they can be as frustrated, frustrating, and dysfunctional as anybody else when their needs are not being met.

Do not expect everyone to want to be a member of the team. Hubs and Blues tend to be more positive toward teams than do either Reds or Greens. Many Hubs feel good about themselves when they can contribute to the team, while Blues can usually be counted on to be helpful and supportive. As the case study of the medical office shows, however, without some insight Hubs and Blues can create as many problems as anyone else. Reds, on the other hand, will be satisfied with teams only if those teams are productive and only if the Red can contribute directly to that productivity. But Greens, in general, do not need nor do they like teams. They can still be of value to the team, however, if their role is to contribute work that they have done on their own to the team effort.

In the concluding chapter of their book on corporate cultures, the authors suggest that the organization of the future will consist primarily of "small, task-focused work units,...each with economic and managerial control over its own destiny, interconnected with larger entities through benign computer and communications links, and bonded into larger companies through strong cultural bonds." If the basic organizational unit of the future will be the relatively small, relatively autonomous work group, then building effective teams will be the equivalent of building effective organizations. As local units become more autonomous and more participatory, the skills of face to face, small group communication will become essential to organizational success. Relationship Awareness Theory can make a powerful contribution to that future.

Deal and Kennedy, *Corporate Cultures*, pp. 182-183.

Understanding Management

Up to this point I have talked as if management were primarily a Red activity, and to the extent that management involves such activities as goal setting, competing, and persuading, such a designation makes some sense. Yet, obviously, there are a variety of ways of managing, and you have probably known many successful managers who were not Red (and probably some unsuccessful ones who were). Relationship Awareness Theory defines not one but four different ways of looking at the process of management.

Management by Enablement (Blue). Managers often find it necessary to clear the way for the successful activities of others. This approach to management involves less leading and directing and more encouraging and supporting. To the extent that a manager is helping his or her people grow and develop in their work he or she is managing by enablement.

Management by Direction (Red). This is the typical or perhaps stereotypical approach to management. Management by direction is particularly appropriate in those situations in which there are clearly defined and commonly accepted goals, clear measures of success, some risk, and, usually, the presence of acknowledged competitors.

Management by Exception (Green). This approach to management is fairly common in relatively large organizations in which the majority of work is done in prescribed or routine ways. The responsibility of management in this situation is to establish very clear guidelines within which everyone operates. Management only becomes actively involved in day to day activities when it encounters a clear deviation, exception, or special case that does not fit within those guidelines.

Management by Participation (Hub). Group participation, employee involvement, opportunities for input, and, frequently, consensus decision making characterize most team management situations. Group problem solving and group decision making demand participation and involvement, particularly where decisions must be carried out under conditions of little or no supervision.

To some extent, of course, we place our own mark on whatever situation we find ourselves in, and Blues, Reds, Greens and Hubs would all perform differently in the same management position. The problem arises when management positions that primarily require one type of behavior are filled by someone with a different orientation. Unless that individual is able to borrow a relating style from the appropriate orientation, he or she will either not be very successful in that position or will need to pay the emotional costs of assuming a "Mask" Relating Style.

Perhaps as difficult are those situations in which there is a mismatch between an individual's performance in a particular management role and the *expectation* others have for that role. If you see your job as one requiring management by enablement, for example, and I expect you to operate through participation, the potential for misunderstanding between us is great. If several people in the same organizational unit have expectations that differ from each other's *and* yours, the likelihood of successful performance is minimal.

Finally, managers and supervisors are the source of organizational rewards. We looked in the last chapter at the idea of how certain rewards are appropriate for certain orientations, and organizations can be far more successful than they normally are in sustaining productive behavior by providing awards that match the orientation of the recipient. Managers can also be more sensitive to the idea that what one orientation finds rewarding may not be rewarding (and may even be punishing) to someone of another orientation. To reward a Green engineer, for instance, with a promotion to department head is only to invite trouble.

At the heart of the management process lies what is called empowerment. We often tend to think of power in organizations as limited. One individual is seen as having some, another little, most none. And to the extent that some people are potentially more influential than others, this is probably appropriate. But another way of looking at power is to think of power as potentially infinite. Power lies within and comes from people. If managers can learn to interact more frequently with each other and with their subordinates in ways that enhance both their own sense of self-worth and that of others, they will have empowered those others and, through them, their organizations.

Understanding Your Job

Hopefully this chapter has given you some better insights into the world of work through your understanding of Relationship Awareness Theory. But how, specifically, do these ideas apply to *your* job? To help answer that question, I would like you to complete the **Job Interactions Inventory** which follows. This inventory will help you assess the kinds of rewards your job has to offer by taking stock of what that job requires in the way of interpersonal relations.

This inventory is completed in the same way you did the **Strength Deployment Inventory**. You are to distribute 10 points among the three endings to show how frequently your job requires the person in that job to act in each of three different ways. Please use all 10 points and never use more or less than 10 points. You may, of course, use zeros if appropriate.

Job Interactions Inventory© copyright 1978, 1989 Personal Strengths Publishing. All rights reserved in the U.S. and elsewhere. This inventory, or parts thereof, may not be reproduced in any form without the prior written permission of the publisher.
Published by Personal Strengths Publishing, Inc.
P.O. Box 2605, Carlsbad CA 92018-2605
(619) 730-7310*
* *New area code will be (760) starting March 1997.*

JOB INTERACTIONS INVENTORY®

Elias H. Porter, Ph.D.

(Rev. 1989)

Job/Position Title _____

Completed by _____ Date _____

DIRECTIONS

This Inventory is designed to help people assess the kinds of rewards that a given job or position has to offer by taking stock of what the job or position requires in the way of interpersonal interactions.

Most jobs require a variety of interpersonal interactions depending upon the circumstances. This Inventory takes this into account in the following manner. Each item in the Inventory starts with an incomplete sentence followed by three different endings. You are to distribute 10 points among the three endings to show how frequently the job requires the person in the job to act in each of the three ways. Always use all 10 points. Never use fewer than 10 points nor more than 10 points. You may use zeros, if they are appropriate, as in the example below.

EXAMPLE

This job requires a person to be...

| 3 | friendly and outgoing as much as possible. | 0 | alert to any and all opportunities. | 7 | very careful before making commitments. |

This is an inventory: not a test. Precision in your answers is not expected. Feel free to change any of your answers until you are reasonably satisfied with them.

©Copyright 1978, 1989 Porter. All rights reserved in the U.S. and elsewhere. This inventory, or parts thereof, may not be reproduced in any form without the prior written permission of Sara E. Maloney.
Published by Personal Strengths Publishing, Inc., P.O. Box 397, Pacific Palisades, CA 90272, (800) 624-SDIS.

1. *This job requires a person to...*

   ☐ be in a helpful, supporting relationship to others throughout the working day.

   ☐ provide direction to, set goals for and motivate the activities of others.

   ☐ be self-reliant and self-directing with minimal guidance by or help from others.

2. *This job is most rewarding to a person who...*

   ☐ enjoys doing things that are of benefit to and help meet the needs of others.

   ☐ is strong, eager and ambitious; a winner; a person who enjoys being the leader of others.

   ☐ is clear and analytic; a person who enjoys thinking things through with precision and logic.

3. *This job will provide opportunity for a person who understands the productivity in...*

   ☐ a concern for the welfare of others and how they are feeling.

   ☐ self-assertion, giving directions and taking over control of what needs to be done.

   ☐ a logical, analytic approach to things and careful planning ahead.

4. *This job appeals most to someone who...*

   ☐ likes to support an effective leader who appreciates and rewards true loyalty.

   ☐ likes to direct the activities of others and to see things accomplished effectively.

   ☐ strives for perfection and enjoys doing things in a precise and orderly manner.

5. *This job requires that a person be...*

   ☐ quick to sense what others need and to give them first priority.

   ☐ quick to see how things can get done and what actions are needed to get started.

   ☐ cautious and careful in reaching any decision on which anyone will have to take action.

☐ Column Total

☐ Column Total

☐ Column Total   *(Sum of columns must equal 50)*

☐ Column 1 Score = Total x 2

☐ Column 2 Score = Total x 2

☐ Column 3 Score = Total x 2   *(Sum of scores must equal 100)*

6. *When a person in this job runs into a new and unexpected situation, the job requires the person to...*

☐ bring it to his or her superior for guidance and decision.

☐ do what seems most likely to succeed and do it *now*.

☐ gather the facts and analyze the issues before taking any action.

7. *When a person in this job must depend upon the cooperation of others to get things done, the job requires the person to...*

☐ place faith in the others and trust that they will do their parts as best they can.

☐ make certain that they understand clearly just exactly what is expected of them.

☐ be prepared with alternatives and backup plans in the event the others don't come through.

8. *When a person in this job encounters a situation where morale is unjustifiably low, the job requires the person to...*

☐ reach out to those involved in an effort to help them reestablish trust.

☐ show them that they are wrong and that their behavior is unproductive.

☐ analyze what went wrong with their thinking and assess how their attitudes might influence his or her own performance.

9. *When a person in this job encounters incompetence in a fellow worker, the job requires the person to...*

☐ do what he or she can to make up for the incompetence so that no one or no part of the work suffers.

☐ confront the person with his or her incompetence and persuade them to do things the right way.

☐ make certain the other person's incompetence is not allowed to interfere with his or her own performance.

10. *In dealing with someone who tends to be uncooperative, the job requires the person to...*

☐ not make trouble but to keep things as harmonious and as tension-free as possible.

☐ find a way to win the person over into being more cooperative.

☐ bypass that person as much as possible and figure out how to get the job done in other ways.

☐ Column Total

☐ Column Total

☐ Column Total   *(Sum of columns must equal 50)*

☐ Column 4 Score = Total x 2

☐ Column 5 Score = Total x 2

☐ Column 6 Score = Total x 2   *(Sum of scores must equal 100)*

Enter your
       JOB INTERACTIONS INVENTORY®
       scores in the boxes to the right —

Col. 1	Col. 2	Col. 3	Col. 4	Col. 5	Col. 6

Enter your
       STRENGTH DEPLOYMENT INVENTORY®
       scores in the boxes to the right —
       INTERPERSONAL INTERACTION TRIANGLE

Col. 1	Col. 2	Col. 3	Col. 4	Col. 5	Col. 6

Plot your Job Interactions Inventory® scores and your Strength Deployment Inventory® (or Personal Values Inventory®) scores on the triangle below. This triangle has been divided into regions labeled as VERY BLUE, BLUE, RED BLUE, etc. If your JII® scores and your SDI® scores plot closely to one another, it seems reasonable to believe that the job demands match your Valued Relating Style. To the extent that the discrepancy between the two becomes substantial, you might use that discrepancy to ask yourself whether there are any parts of your job which push you into the necessity of using a lot of a Borrowed Style or even a Mask Style.

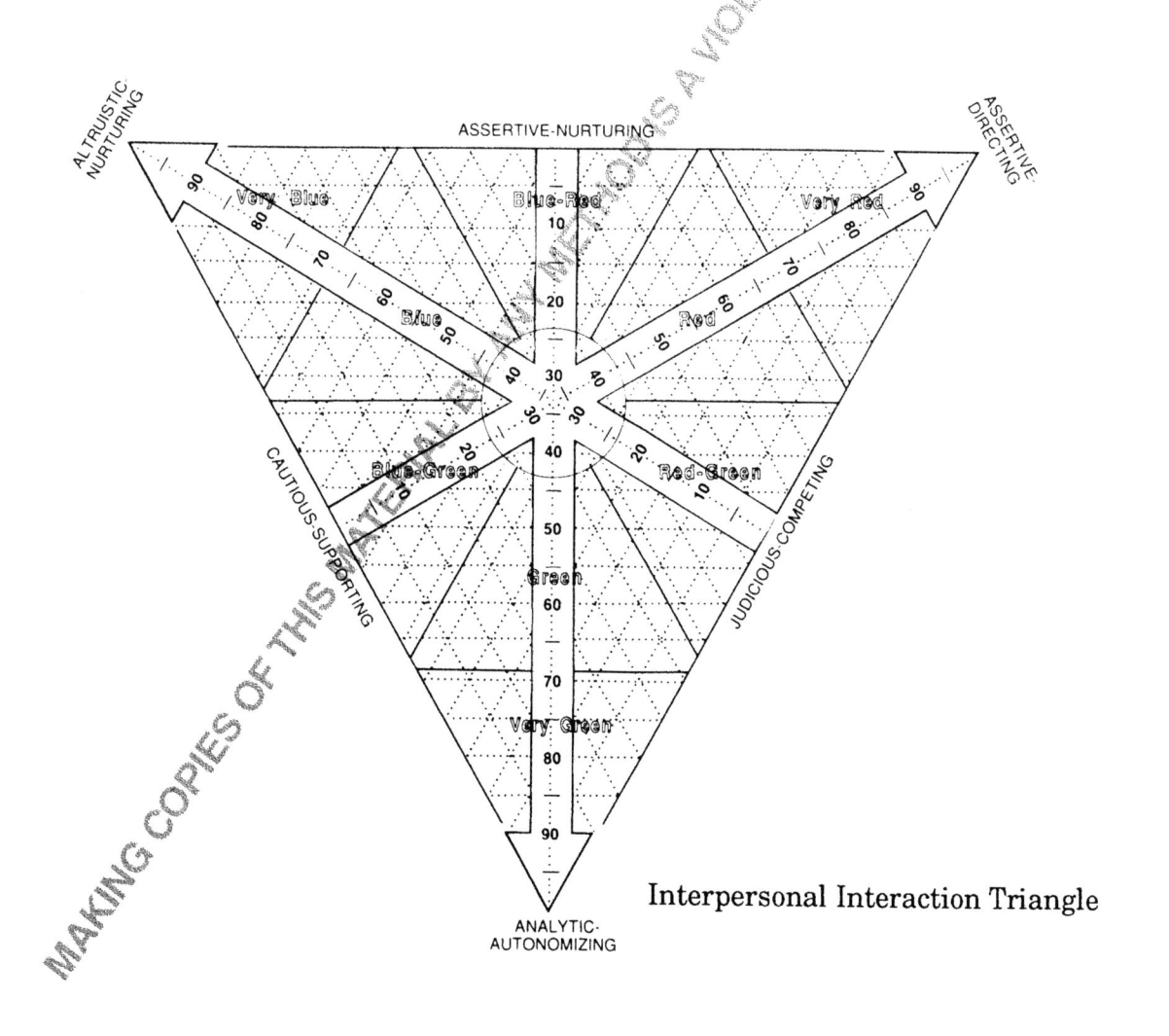

Interpersonal Interaction Triangle

Copies of the JOB INTERACTIONS INVENTORY® may be ordered from:
Personal Strengths Publishing, Inc., P.O. Box 397, Pacific Palisades, California 90272 (800) 624-SDIS

At this point, plot your scores from the **Job Interactions Inventory** in the space provided on the previous page. If the scores on the two instruments plot closely to each other, it seems reasonable to believe that the job matches your valued relating style. To the extent that the discrepancy between the two becomes substantial, you might explore the extent to which your job requires you to use a Borrowed or even "Mask" Relating Style.

In doing this you may find it helpful to look at your scores on the two instruments one at a time, comparing your Blue score on each instrument, your Red score, and then your Green score. Scores that are within six points of each other should be treated as equal. If the scores differ by twelve or more points that difference may be worth some real study in your analysis of what behaviors your job rewards or does not reward.

Remember, the **Job Interactions Inventory** is not a precise measure or test of the differences between your valued relating style and the behavior required by your job but is meant to help you raise questions about how well your job fits you. Some questions you might want to consider are:

> "When all is going well for you on the job, are you free to act in the ways that most gratify you?"
>
> "Are there some aspects of the job you must 'put up with' but don't really like?"
>
> "Does the job require you to 'put up a front' that is really not like you?"
>
> "What are the parts of your job you find most rewarding?"
>
> "What parts of your job do you find least rewarding or even irksome?"
>
> "When you are faced with conflict on the job, can you meet that conflict in ways that are natural for you or are you forced to play a role that is unlike you?"

Record your thoughts or responses to these questions in the space provided.

```
_____
_____
_____
_____
```

Next, take a look at the organization in which this job takes place. The following table identifies ten strengths associated with each orientation. For each strength, identify by a check mark (✔) your perception of the extent to which it is "rewarded," "expected but not rewarded," "disregarded," or "punished" in your organization. Think of each of these categories in the following ways:

Rewarded: A strongly valued strength or behavior, one for which an individual will find himself or herself rewarded or praised.

Expected but not rewarded: A strength or behavior that is assumed or taken for granted but not particularly rewarded.

Disregarded: A strength or behavior that is ignored but not singled out for punishment.

Punished: A negatively valued strength or behavior, one for which an individual will find himself or herself in trouble or punished.

Blue	Rewarded	Expected but not Rewarded	Disregarded	Punished	**Green**	Rewarded	Expected but not Rewarded	Disregarded	Punished
Trusting					Cautious				
Optimistic					Practical				
Loyal					Economical				
Idealistic					Reserved				
Helpful					Methodical				
Modest					Analytic				
Devoted					Thorough				
Caring					Orderly				
Supportive					Fair				
Accepting					Persevering				
TOTALS					TOTALS				

Red	Rewarded	Expected but not Rewarded	Disregarded	Punished	Hub	Rewarded	Expected but not Rewarded	Disregarded	Punished
Self-confident					Flexible				
Enterprising					Open to change				
Ambitious					Social				
Organizer					Experimenter				
Persuasive					Curious				
Forceful					Adaptable				
Quick to act					Tolerant				
Imaginative					Open to compromise				
Competitive					Looks for options				
Risk-taking					Team player				
TOTALS					TOTALS				

On the basis of your scores from the **Strength Deployment Inventory** and the **Job Interactions Inventory** and your analysis of the extent to which your organization rewards or punishes certain behaviors, you may wish to consider the following questions:

"When all is going well for you on the job, is there a good match between your interpersonal orientation and the demands of the organization?"

"When all is going well for you on the job, is there a good match between the behavior demanded by your job and the demands of the organization?"

"What problems do you see in the match between your orientation, the demands of your job and the demands of the organization?"

"What changes could you initiate right now to improve that match?"

Record your thoughts to these questions in the space provided below.

_____
_____
_____
_____

Hopefully, you will have found a reasonably good match between your valued relating style, the behavior demanded by your job, and the behavior rewarded by your organization. If that match does not exist, perhaps you have been able to identify something you might actually do to improve that situation.

Of course, if as a result of this analysis you have identified a significant lack of fit between your current position or organization, if you have been unable to identify any constructive changes you might make in this situation, or if you have found that you have been forced to adopt a "Mask" Relating Style in this situation, some serious reconsideration of how you are making your living might be in order.

Conclusion

Various polls from time to time report that a significant number of us are unhappy with our jobs. Relationship Awareness Theory would suggest that a major reason is that too often, our jobs do not provide us with enough opportunities to do the kind of things that enhance our sense of self-worth and allow us to feel good about ourselves as people. I hope you have found that this is not the case with you, or that there are some things you can do to improve your situation. If, however, you have found yourself in a job or organization that does not enhance your feelings of self-worth, I hope you will have the courage to change that situation. Life, as they say, is far too short to spend it in ways that do not allow us to feel worthwhile about ourselves.

Chapter Eight

Using Relationship Awareness Theory

At the beginning of this book, I suggested that the primary value of Relationship Awareness Theory would be the extent to which you found these ideas of practical value to you. I trust that you now have a fuller understanding of yourself and others, and of yourself in relation to others. The purpose of this final chapter is to look at some real life applications of these ideas.

Summarizing Relationship Awareness Theory

First, let's summarize some of the basic assumptions and ideas contained in Relationship Awareness Theory.

> *All persons want to feel worthwhile about themselves.* The single most important idea in Relationship Awareness Theory is that every person is like all other people in that everyone wants to feel valuable and worthwhile about themselves. Interpersonal interactions are best understood as attempts by the individuals involved to achieve or enhance their feelings of self-worth. The fact that some people are more successful at this than others in no way negates the validity of this idea.
>
> *Every person has a unifying value system.* Every person has a set of beliefs which he or she uses to direct and evaluate his or her interactions with other people. On the basis of this value system, each person determines the extent to which an interaction has enhanced or diminished his or her sense of worth as a human being.
>
> *A Valued Relating Style is a person's characteristic way of behaving when he or she is free to act in ways that make him or her feel worthwhile.* When a person is free to act in a way that makes him or her feel worthwhile, he or she uses his or her Valued Relating Style. A Valued Relating Style is the style we associate with a person as his or her personality or characteristic way of behaving.
>
> *A Borrowed Relating Style can be used in pursuit of a desired goal.* This is a style of relating in which the

behavior as such does not enhance feelings of self-worth but which can be used to achieve the same goal as that sought by an individual's Valued Relating Style. In a borrowed relating style, one's behavior has changed but not one's underlying purpose.

A non-valued or "Mask" Relating Style does not help an individual feel good about himself or herself. This is a style of relating that a person learns to put on like a mask because it is expected, required, or needed for survival. Not only does the use of a Mask Relating Style not help an individual feel worthwhile, but also long-term or continued use of such a style may significantly erode an individual's sense of self-worth.

In the face of conflict, behavior may change. Conflict, in Relationship Awareness Theory, is defined as any relationship or situation in which we are blocked from achieving the objectives associated with our Valued Relating Style. Our response to conflict is then best understood as an attempt to defend our sense of self-worth and to change the conflict situation to one in which we can again feel good about ourselves.

As we have seen, there are four primary orientations—Blue, Red, Green, and Hub—and three blends of motivations—Red-Blue, Red-Green, and Blue-Green. Although our Valued Relating Style can be defined in these terms, there are no pure types, only differences in priorities. Everyone, under circumstances unique to the individual, wants to be of honest help to someone, wants to step in and run the show, wants to be left alone to do things in his or her own way, and wants to be flexible and keep his or her options open. Everyone has some of each motivation, and all of us have been, at one time or another, Blue or Red or Green or Hub. There can be no doubt, however, that each of us feels most worthwhile when we can act in ways that are consistent with our Valued Relating Style.

Applying Relationship Awareness Theory

One of the important things about Relationship Awareness Theory is that it leads to new discoveries. Once you understand the basic concepts, you can use those concepts to create new ideas, new insights. At this point, you should be in a position to apply Relationship Awareness Theory to a wide variety of personal and professional situations. Let me suggest a few ways these ideas can be used to illuminate various aspects of our lives.

Conflict management. Some conflicts are unwarranted and should not exist. Others are real but can be resolved through negotiation and compromise. Others are also very real, but if they involve deeply held values, perhaps should not be resolved. Relationship Awareness Theory can help us understand, manage, and, where appropriate, resolve a wide variety of interpersonal conflicts.

Time management. Each interpersonal orientation is subject to different time management problems and requires different time management solutions. Planning, scheduling, and prioritizing, the heart of traditional time management, will be handled quite differently by Blues, Reds, Greens, and Hubs. A powerful goal-oriented time management program may be quite appropriate for Reds but quite inappropriate for other orientations.

Career development. Careers are best thought of as a continual process of matching the needs and values of the individual with the needs and values of the job. Relationship Awareness Theory can help us to understand more clearly those needs and values and to identify with greater clarity those matches and mismatches.

Sales training. Sales is generally considered to be a Red profession. But what if those Reds are trying to sell laboratory equipment to Green technicians? Relationship Awareness Theory provides a whole new way of looking at prospects and creating sales strategies appropriate to different orientations.

You should now have enough mastery of Relationship Awareness Theory to explore for yourself the implications of these ideas for such issues as customer relations, family counseling, leadership and supervisory development, performance review, life planning and marital relations. An entire book could probably be written about each of these topics. Once you have understood these ideas, you will find yourself writing your own book on Relationship Awareness Theory every day as you apply these concepts to your own job and to your own personal and professional relationships. There is no end to the journey, just the journey itself. We can constantly use the insights and concepts of Relationship Awareness Theory to increase our understanding of our own unfolding journey.

Chapter Eight

Relationship Awareness Theory and You

In this book, you have been asked to reflect on and write about certain aspects of Relationship Awareness Theory. Those parts of the book may be the most important for you. They ask you to apply these ideas to your understanding of yourself and your relationships with others. To begin pulling these ideas together for yourself, take a few moments to review what you have written in each of the previous chapters, then complete the following statements:

The most important thing I have learned about myself from Relationship Awareness Theory:

_____
_____
_____
_____
_____
_____

The most important thing I have learned about interpersonal relations from Relationship Awareness Theory:

_____
_____
_____
_____
_____
_____

Relationship Awareness Theory will be of value for you only to the extent that it helps improve your relationships with others. Hopefully these summary reflections will have helped you focus in on the significance of these ideas for you.

Conclusion

Every day, each of us is faced with numerous opportunities to interact with other people. Sometimes in those interactions we behave in ways that enhance both our own sense of self-worth and the sense of self-worth of others. Too often, however, we find ourselves acting in ways that undermine or damage our own feelings of worth or the feelings of worth of others.

Given our current understanding of human behavior, it is not possible to behave in ways that, one hundred percent of the time, will enhance our sense of self-worth and the sense of self-worth of others. Relationship Awareness Theory can, however, increase our batting average. Through an understanding of our own orientation and the orientation of others, we can become more *intentional* in our actions with others, which simply means that what we want to have happen as a result of that interaction happens more frequently.

If we choose, each of us can create more mutually gratifying relationships. Relationship Awareness Theory, as developed over the last thirty years by Dr. Elias Porter, can help each of us create better, more productive human relations. The tools are now in your hands. The choice is up to you.

Appendix A

Relationship Awanesss Theory
By Dr. Elias H. Porter

(Note: this is a letter written by Dr. Porter to the British distritutor of the Strength Deployment Inventory, Mr. Michael C. Gallon. It was published in the publication TRAINING OFFICER in the UK in December of 1983. It is reproduced here to offer further insights into the nature of Relationship Awareness Theory.)

Mr. Michael C. Gallon, Director
Personal Strengths Publishing (UK) Ltd.
22 St. Peters Road
Oundle
Peterborough PE8 4NS — England

Dear Mike,

You ask me to summarize the latest developments in Relationship Awareness Theory so that the readers of Training Officer may be brought up to date.

The greatest effort has been directed toward helping people to *not misuse* the theory.

Where most theories of personal behaviour are based on typologies of *behaviour*, Relationshp Awareness Theory is based on a typology of *motivations*. A rough analogy is in the difference between the first generation of bicycles and the second generation of bicycles. The first generation of bicycles had two wheels, a frame, a seat and handle bars for steering: power to propel was provided by pushing with one's legs as with a Kiddie Kar. The second generation bicycle added pedals, sprockets and chains: power to propel came from a circular movement of the legs much as in walking. The potential for effectiveness as a transportation device is clearly greater in the second generation bicycle but only if the rider learns to use the pedals. If the rider chooses not to use the pedals and chooses to push along in Kiddie Kar fashion, he forfeits the potential for greater effectiveness.

If one chooses to use a theory of interpersonal relationships that is based on a typology of motivation as though it were based on a typology of behaviour, one chooses to forfeit a large measure of the additional effectiveness available through a typology of motivation. On the other hand, if one chooses to avail one's self of the additional effectiveness, one must learn to put aside the old

"Kiddie-Kar-push-along" skills and learn to use the pedals instead.

At this point, the obvious question is, "What are the 'Kiddie-Kar-push-along' skills you refer to?"

The more primitive skills I refer to are involved when a person says, "Oh, he's a Blue, he'll want to help," or "He's a Red so he will want to be in charge," or "He's a Green, he'll want to analyze it." In each case the interpreter has inferred from a general truth as though it were a universal truth.

Just because our first individual above is a True-Blue by all measures, by all observation and by self-description does not at all mean "he'll want to help." As a matter of fact, knowing that he is a Blue may be the basis for prediction that in a given instance he would not want to help. To learn to use the pedals one must learn to predict individual responses on the basis of what the individual wants as an outcome. Blues want their behaviour to result in benefit to others: they may accomplish this by "helping" behaviour, if that is appropriate, or by saying "no", if the refusal to "help" is the best way to benefit the other.

The Red may in no way want to "be in charge" if there are no tasks to be accomplished, no resources to be managed, no authority given on which to act, or no responsibility assigned to achieve some goal. On the other hand, give a Red a serious task to accomplish, the authority to accomplish it, the resources he needs to get the task done and you might well see that Red bending over backward to be directly helpful to someone who is a key person on the road to success. Again, to learn to use the pedals, one must learn to predict individual responses on the basis of what behaviour in the situation is appropriate to what the individual wants as an outcome. Reds want to get the job done whether they have to "lead, follow or get the hell out of the way!"

The Greens are certainly not going to waste their time, their energy or any of their other resources on putting into order that which is already in order. You might see a Green being very assertive in a relationship in support of a proved procedure. Once again, to use the pedals one must understand the outcomes people want to achieve.

Over the years I have come to appreciate the futility of telling people what not to do. I can tell people to quit trying to predict behaviour from behavioural stereotypes and have about the same degree of success as telling them not to think of a red hat on top of a fence post. As a consequence I have recently tried to forge and supply people with the kinds of conceptual tools that help them to focus in a constructive way on the relationship between behavioural styles and the outcomes people want to achieve. My efforts have resulted in the following definitions.

Style Of Relating. A style of relating is any identifiable pattern of overt behaviour in which a person engages to reach a certain goal which the individual wants to reach or is forced to reach by reason of circumstance. All of us know that we engage in different identifiable patterns of overt bahavious under different circumstances. We may be ecstatically happy and joyous when the home team wins the game and we seek to share with others and have them share with us the exhilaration we all feel. We may be politeness itself in dealing with a boorish customer. We act to achieve ends. Any pattern of overt acts which are directed toward an end we can rightly call a style of relating.

Basic Value System. A person's basic value system is the set of values one holds by which one judges whether the goals one strives for are good goals (and make one feel good and worthwhile as a person), whether the goals one strives for are bad goals (and make one feel negatively about one's self) or whether the goals one strives for are somewhere in between being good or bad.

Given that all of us like to feel good about ourselves as persons, yet find ourselves from time to time engaging in behaviour we don't approve of in ourselves and make us feel anywhere from not so good to feeling rotten about ourselves, we can identify three quite different kinds of relating styles directly related to our value systems, the goals we pursue, the things we want as outcomes of our behaviour.

The first of these is the Valued Relating Style. This is the style of relating to others one most often likes to follow because most of the time it makes one feel good about one's self to act that way. And it is because the Valued Relating Style is the most frequently employed means of seeking to produce the outcome the person wants to produce: its sheer frequency makes it the most noticeable and the most "characteristic" pattern of behaviour the individual evidences. (Most schemes for identifying leadership styles, personalities, temperment styles, selling styles, marital relations styles, power styles and numerous other styles are based principally on the observation of the consistencies in behaviour of Valued Relating Styles.) This consistency in behaviour is both a blessing and a curse. It gives us a very valuable base for predicting much of an individual's behaviour yet at the same time it tempts us to fall into the trap of stereotyping and predicting that because the individual behaves in "this way" as a general rule he or she will behave in "this way" in specific instances without stopping to ask ourselves whether or not that particular style of behaving is most likely to produce the outcome the person wants to produce.

Which leads us to an apparent paradox: the use of an "uncharacterisitc" style of relating to achieve what one "characteristically" wants as an outcome. I call this a Borrowed Relating Style, a style of relating that by itself wouldn't make a person feel good about self but is an acceptable style because it is used to produce a valued outcome. We need only think of the nurturant teacher who runs a classroom with an iron hand in order to be more helpful to her pupils, or the industrialist who develops an elaborate employee benefit plan as a means to assure the loyalty of his employees. The Borrowed Relating Style may differ markedly, and sometimes dramatically, from the person's most characteristic or Valued Relating Style, yet the outcome the person wants to achieve may be identical.

At this point we come to yet a third set of human experiences which help us to see the validity of an additional definition, the definition of Non-Valued Relating Styles.

There are times in our lives when we do not have the luxury of relating to others in ways that make us feel good about ourselves. We may, for example, find that our job requires us to act in ways we don't value and we must seek personal fulfillment outside of the work place. And what often complicates our lives even more is when the world tells us we should like what we are doing when in fact it may hold little for us in the way of self-fullfilment. Someone has called many women "unwilling victims" of motherhood. A mother who is a real green, for example, may love her child most deeply but be terribly burdened and only marginally rewarded by the seemingly endless demands for nurturance the child presents year after year.

It is certainly my most fervent hope that those brave souls who undertake to expose themselves to Relationship Awareness Theory will be able to avoid the obvious pitfalls of stereotyping people on the basis of their Valued Relating Styles and become adept at looking more carefully at people's behaviour patterns and to verify whether the pattern they are observing—and upon which they are basing their predictions—is a Valued Relating Style, a Borrowed Relating Style or a Non-Valued Relating Style: it could affect their predictions most markedly.

One of Murphy's Laws advises, "The race is Not Always to the Swift Nor the Battle to the Strong: But that's the Way to Bet."

I can tell you one thing—I would bet on neither the Swift nor the Strong, if I judged their hearts were not in the contest. And Relationship Awareness Theory, better than any other theory I know of, helps one to see where the other person's heart is.

Elias H. Porter

Appendix B

On the Development of Relationship Awareness Theory: A Personal Note
by Dr. Elias H. Porter

Relationship Awareness Theory is based on the premise that one's behavior traits are consistent with what one finds gratifying in interpersonal relations and with concepts or beliefs one holds about how to interact with others to achieve those gratifications. Although many personality theories are about people, this theory was meant for people. It was intended to provide an effective means for understanding one's self and for understanding others so that interpersonal relationships could be mutually productive and gratifying. The theory was planned to help people organize their concepts of themselves and their concepts of others around three basic motivations: wanting to be of genuine help to others, wanting to be the leader of others, and wanting to be self-reliant and self-dependent.

In the mid-1930's, I was fortunate enough to be a student of Calvin S. Hall and Robert W. Leeper. Hall had just completed his doctoral studies with the late Edward C. Tolman at the University of California at Berkeley, so, of course, I became immersed in the concepts of purposive behavior, latent learning, hypothesis formation, and the factor of emphasis in learning. Leeper had been heavily influenced by Kurt Lewin, so I also became immersed in field theory. Under their tutelege, I rejected as too simplistic any efforts to understand human behavior in terms of pairings of stimuli to responses or responses to stimuli. Any model of human behavior, it seemed to me, had to include consideration for differential motivation to account for why we seek certain stimuli at one time and other stimuli at another time. It must also include consideration of concept formation as an important intervening variable between motivation and response.

In the late 1930's when I studied with Carl Rogers, I learned to perceive how another human being was conceptualizing his world of experience. In today's slang, I was learning how "to get into people's heads." Even more important, I learned that as human beings become more sharply aware of their own motivations and more sharply aware of their conceptualizations of how to be in this world, their concepts change, and new behaviors appropriate to the new concepts replace old behavior patterns.

My first opportunity to apply this new learning was when I was named merit system supervisor for the Oregon State Public Welfare Commission just prior to World War II. To select public assistance workers, I developed an eight-hour test designed to assess the extent to which an individual tended to conceptualize the "helping process" as one in which one could help most by telling the person what he should do, by telling the person about his weaknesses, by giving reassurance, by asking probing questions, or by providing empathic understanding. I identified some of the important tasks a public assistance worker would have to perform and then built test items from the conceptual framework of (1) a moralistic person, who knew what people ought to do, (2) an interpretive person, who knew what insights the client ought to have, (3) a reassurance-giving person, who knew what it was to suffer, (4) a probing person, who always needed a bit more information, and (5) an empathic person, who could be with the individual as the individual experienced himself at each moment. I was surprised at the high degrees of internal consistency that almost all of the test items yielded when analyzed. This was true no matter what work setting was used. But I could not connect these consistencies in conceptual patterns with any underlying motivations, and I was unwilling to take the position that behind any detectable consistency in conceptualization lies a special motivation.

In 1949 I read *Man for Himself* (Fromm, 1947). I was intrigued with Fromm's treatment of Freud's assumption that behavior flows from how one's character is organized. Fromm saw the manner in which character is organized as stemming from certain motivations. Here was a more complete model: first comes motivation, then character organization, and, finally, behavior.

At that time, the prevailing concept of mental health was the absence of psychopathology. Although Fromm alluded to "productivity" in his writing, he treated it in a very general manner—as an expression of the power of loving and the power of thinking. On the other hand, he was explicit about what he called the "nonproductive orientations." He identified (1) the receptive orientation, based on the need to receive from others; (2) the exploitative orientation, based on the need to take from others; (3) the hoarding orientation, based on the need to preserve from others; and (4) the marketing orientation, based on an alienation from one's own potentials and the need to be connected with other people in whatever manner they can accept.

Because I was working with a "clinical population," I began with the nonproductive orientations. My aim was to develop a questionnaire that could be given to counselees to assess how they saw themselves (both negatively and positively) in terms of behavior traits representative of the four orientations. Over the next few years, the questionnaire took on several different forms. As the concept of personal congruence began to take form, I designed into one form of the questionnaire items that described one's intentions, items that described how one acted, and items that described the emotional impact one made on others. Before I had a chance to assess the validity of these items, I accepted another position in research, and my clinical records went into the files.

Some twelve years later, in 1971, I returned to my questionnaire with a fresh view. I had become quite interested in the notion of heuristics—ideas, concepts, or models that lead to discovery. (When everyone knew that the world was flat, the idea that the world was round served as a heuristic device; it led people to new discoveries). I wanted to redesign my questionnaire to assess only a person's strengths in relating to others, rather that to discover pathologies. I felt this would serve as an effective heuristic device.

I did not consider the "marketing orientation," for in Fromm's words, "The marketing orientation, however, does not develop something which is potentially in the person (unless we make the absurd assertion that 'nothing' is also part of the human equipment); its very nature is that no specific and permanent kind of relatedness is developed, but that the very changeability of attitudes is the only permanent quality of such orientation" (p.84).

I titled the new questionnaire the Strength Deployment Inventory and set about determining the internal consistency of the items. I administered the inventory until I had enough subjects to do an item analysis. After several rewrites, I was satisfied with the instrument and published it in its present form.

When I administered the inventory, I shared with the subjects what their scores might mean about how they tended to behave and what behavior traits seemed to be characteristic for them. Repeatedly, people explained to me why they behaved as they did. They gave me their reasons for acting in one way or another. And these reasons had to do with what they wanted from their relationships.

Finally, I rediscovered what I had learned earlier: behavior flows from conceptual orientation, and conceptual orientation flows from systems of strivings. But the strivings that people talked about, the strivings as they experienced them, were not described in the sexual terms that Freud used nor were they described in the terms that Fromm proposed. Individuals who predominantly displayed those behavior traits that Fromm associated with the receptive orientation (the striving to be given to) reported their major striving was to be genuinely helpful to and nurturant of others. They had little or no concern for what they received in return. I renamed this striving the Altruistic-Nurturing motivation. Individuals who predominantly displayed those behavior traits that Fromm associated with the exploitative orientation (the striving to take from others) reported their major concern was to be leaders of others but not at others' expense. I called this striving Assertive-Directing. Individuals who predominantly displayed those behavior traits that Fromm associated with the hoarding orientation (the striving for infinite security) reported their major concerns with logic and analysis to create order and achieve self-reliance and self-dependence (not independence) as their way of relating to their fellow men. I named this striving the Analytic-Autonomizing motivation.

As I began to conceive of these strivings as strivings for positive values, the quality of my interpretations of the inventory scores began to change and so did the responses to my interpretations. I was convinced that I had produced a better heuristic device that could help lead people to self-discovery.

Another experience I had may extend Relationship Awareness Theory into the field of pathological behavior. I introduced the theory to a small group of psychiatric technicians in charge of mentally ill offenders in a mental hospital. On one ward was a man who had been charged with murder and declared too disturbed to stand trial. He was described by the technicians as argumentative and a troublemaker; he was considered potentially dangerous to other patients and to staff personnel. This patient completed the Strength Deployment Inventory. The technicians, as one might anticipate, predicted that he would score highest on the Assertive-Directing scale. The opposite was true. He scored lowest on the Assertive-Directing scale when "all was going well" and scored even lower on the Assertive-Directing scale when "faced with conflict and opposition." His highest scores were on the Altruistic-Nurturing scale under both conditions. The technicians decided that either the man had deliberately misrepresented himself or that the instrument was "no damn good." I was puzzled, but the man's scores on the Assertive-Directing scale were very close to mine under both conditions; I know that when all is going well, I do not want to be in the position of directing the activity of others, and when faced with conflict and opposition, the last thing I want to do is to stand up and fight for my rights. I can do it, but the results are likely to be explosive. I am just not calibrated for self-assertion; it tends to be "no go" for an insufferable period of time and then "go for the jugular" as a last resort, with nothing between. I explained this to the technicians. They conjectured that this might possibly be true of their patient. Two months later they told me that they had been treating the man as a person who wanted to be of help around the ward and that his behavior on the ward had improved to the point where he was transferred to the next higher ward.

Assuredly, this is but one case, and the man's improvement could be due to any number of other things, but it does raise the questions of whether pathological behavior is a result of a person's being forced into motivations he does not want and for which his behavior is poorly calibrated and whether that pathological behavior will be abandoned if a person finds gratification of his primary strivings. These questions cannot be answered at this time.

Statement of Theory

Relationship Awareness Theory is a theory of interpersonal relationships rather than a theory of intrapsychic relationships (although the theory promises to bring a new view to the phenomenon we call personality).

First Premise. The first major premise of the theory is that behavior traits are not conditioned responses or reinforced behaviors, as B.F. Skinner would imply, nor are they "primary personality factors" as Raymond Cattell stated (1971). The theory assumes, as does Tolman's theory, that behavior traits arise from purposive strivings for gratification mediated by concepts or hypotheses as to how to obtain those gratifications (Tolman, 1967). Put in simplest terms, behavior traits are the consistencies in our behavior that stem from the consistencies in what we find gratifying in interpersonal relationships and the consistencies in our beliefs or concepts as to how to interact with other people in order to achieve those gratifications.

As we become increasingly aware of the gratifications we are seeking from others and examine our beliefs and concepts as to the best way to achieve those gratifications, we open ourselves to feedback on the efficacy of the behavior in which we engage, with the result that old patterns of behavior may be readily modified or even abandoned for more effective behavior patterns.

As we become increasingly aware of the gratifications that others are seeking from us, their behavior becomes more understandable to us and opens new avenues for the achievement of mutual gratification and the avoidance of unwarranted conflict that may arise when one person presumes that another equally shares his beliefs and motivations.

Relationship Awareness Theory avoids the unspoken assumption underlying so many approaches to understanding human behavior that the world impinges upon the individual in a more or less uniform and undifferentiated manner so that, if one is able to assess an individual's "primary personality factor," one is able to predict, within the error of measurement, the pattern of the individual's behavior in most, if not all, situations. Relationship Awareness Theory holds this assumption, so often left unspoken, to be faulty and misleading.

Second Premise. As a second major premise, Relationship Awareness Theory holds that there are, at the very least, two clear, distinguishably different conditions in the stimulus world that affect patterns of behavior. One of these conditions exists when we are free to pursue the gratifications we seek from others. The second condition exists when we are faced with conflict and opposition so that we are not free to pursue our gratifications but must resort to the preservation of our own integrity and self-esteem. The behavior traits we exhibit under these two conditions truly differ. When we are free to pursue our gratifications, we are more or less uniformly predictable, but in the face of continuing conflict and opposition we undergo changes in motivations that link into different bodies of beliefs and concepts that are, in turn, expressed in yet different behavior traits. We are predictably uniform in our behavior when we are free, and we are predictably variable as we meet with obstructing conditions in our stimulus worlds.

Third Premise. The third major premise is directly from Fromm: a personal weakness is no more, nor no less, than the over-doing of a personal strength. An individual operates from personal "strength" when he behaves in a manner that enhances the probability that an interpersonal interaction will be a mutually productive interaction. An individual operates from personal "weakness" when he behaves in a way that decreases the probability that an interpersonal interaction will be a mutually productive interaction. To act in a trusting manner is a strength; it enhances the probability of mutual productivity. To act in an overly trusting or gullible manner is a weakness; it decreases the probability of mutual productivity and increases the probability of a destructive or, at least, a nonproductive outcome for one or even both of the individuals concerned. The same things can be said for being self-confident and its nonproductive form, being overly self-confident or arrogant. To be cautious is a strength; to be overly cautious or suspicious is a weakness.

When the premise that behavior traits are purposive strivings for gratification is coupled with the premise that weaknesses are strengths overdone, a new dimension in understanding is open to us as facilitators. Whether a given individual is operating from his strengths or from his weaknesses, we should be able to assess the gratifications for which he is striving and, as psychotherapists or facilitators, help the individual assess the effectiveness of his beliefs and concepts about how to interact with other people to obtain the gratification he seeks.

Fourth Premise. A fourth premise relates to two distinctions that can be made among personality theories. First, the concepts inherent in some theories are remote and distant from how one experiences one's self, but the concepts inherent in other theories approximate how one experiences one's self. The second distinction is that in some theories the concepts used amount to labels, while in other theories the concepts lead to further self-discovery.

Eric Erickson, in *Childhood and Society* (1974), writes, "In introjection we feel *and act as if* [emphasis mine] an outer goodness had become an inner certainty. In projection, we experience an inner harm as an outer one: we endow significant people with the evil which actually is in us." I intend in no way to discount the validity of Erickson's assertion, but I do want to point out that the person who is engaged in introjection or in projection does not experience himself as doing so. These concepts are distant from immediate experience. For example, when I am engaging in projection, I need to have someone point out and more or less prove to me that I am projecting. The concept of projection does not serve me very well as a heuristic device; it does not lead me to much self-discovery. It may have heuristic value to me as a facilitator or therapist observing and discovering the behavior of others, however.

Transactional Analysis offers a set of concepts much closer to how we experience ourselves, which serve as rather effective devices for self-discovery. One can rather readily grasp the concepts of "Parent," "Adult," "Child," and "transactions" and understand many of one's relationships with others in these terms. These more experience-proximate concepts not only lead more readily to self-discovery but also point to what can be done to change one's behavior for more effective interpersonal relationships.

The fourth premise, then, is simply that the more clearly the concepts in a personality theory approximate how one experiences one's self, the more effectively they serve as devices for self-discovery. The more a personality theory can be for a person rather than about a person, the better it will serve that person. By implication, were the concepts in personality theory sufficiently close to how we experience ourselves, psychotherapists might well become trainers and the concepts become the healers. I don't think we are there, as yet, but I think the concepts in Relationship Awareness Theory are closer to that possibility than Fromm's concepts of receptive, exploitative, hoarding, and marketing orientations, closer than Karen Horney's concepts of moving toward others, moving against others, and moving from others (Horney, 1950), and closer than the concepts of Parent, Adult, and Child of Transactional Analysis.

Experience-Proximate Concepts

The first set of experience-proximate concepts in Relationship Awareness Theory relates to the first premise, that behavior traits are purposive strivings for gratification. According to the theory, there are three distinguishably different basic strivings in relating to others. The first is the striving to be nurturant of another—wanting to be genuinely helpful to the other person and to see the other person do well—and we all experience ourselves as wanting to be helpful in some of our relationships. The second is the striving to be in the position of directing events—to set goals and be the leader—and we all experience at times wanting to be the person in charge. The third is the striving for autonomy, self-reliance, and self-sufficiency, and we all experience at times wanting to do things for ourselves without help or direction from others. For some individuals, one of these motivations may be predominant.

The second set of concepts relates to the second premise, that there are two distinguishably different conditions in the stimulus world that affect patterns of behavior. When an individual is free to pursue his gratifications, the nurturant motivation takes the form of actively seeking to be helpful to others, the directive motivation takes the form of self-assertion and seeking opportunity to provide leadership (in the conventional sense of leadership), and the autonomizing motivation takes the form of actively seeking logical orderliness and self-reliance.

In the face of conflict and opposition, the nurturant motivation is expressed in efforts to preserve and restore harmony, the directive motivation is expressed in efforts to prevail over the other person, and the autonomizing motivation is expressed in efforts to conserve resources and assure independence.

The third set of concepts is based on the third premise, that a weakness is the overdoing of a strength. Here the concepts are those of actual overdoing and perceived overdoing of strengths. The actual overdoing of a trait, for example, is trusting to the point of being gullible, being self-confident to the point of being arrogant, being cautious to the point of being suspicious, and so on. Perceived overdoing occurs, for example, when someone in whom the nurturing motivation is high interacts with someone in whom the directing motivation is high. When the latter acts quickly with self-confidence, ambition, and directness, the highly nurturant person may well perceive him as arrogant, aggressive, overbearing, and rash. Perceived overdoing is somewhat akin to projection as described by Erickson, but it seems to be more overreacting to behavior in others that would be considered inappropriate for one's self.

The fourth set of concepts is based on the fourth premise, that when the concepts in a personality theory are more closely related to how we experience ourselves, they serve as more effective heuristic devices for self-discovery as well as for understanding the behavior of others. For example, if one knows where he is "coming from" (the gratifications he seeks) and knows where another person is "coming from" (the gratifications the other person seeks), he may assess whether a conflict is unwarranted or real. If it is unwarranted, he may devise strategies for achieving win-win (mutually gratifying) solutions; if the conflict is real, he may attempt to develop a limited relationship or decide to terminate the relationship. Whatever one decides to do may be done with insight and without violating his integrity or the integrity of the other person.

Relationship Awareness Theory seeks to provide first and foremost an effective means to understanding one's self and understanding others, to the end that interpersonal interactions may be made as mutually productive and gratifying as possible or, where they cannot be mutually productive, that destructiveness of individual integrity be minimized.

References

Cattell, R.B. *Abilities: Their Structure, Growth and Action.* Boston: Houghton-Mifflin, 1971.

Erickson, E. *Childhood and Society.* New York: W.W. Norton, 1974.

Fromm, E. *Man For Himself.* New York: Holt, Rinehart, and Winston, 1947.

Horney, K. *Neurosis and Human Growth.* New York: W.W. Norton, 1950.

Tolman, E.C. *Purposive Behavior in Animals and Men.* New York: Irvington Books, 1967.

Elias H. Porter received his Ph. D. degree at Ohio State University in 1941, studying under Carl Rogers. He held teaching posts at the University of Oregon, Ohio State University, the University of Chicago, and the University of California at San Diego and at Los Angeles. He served as associate clinical professor in the Department of Psychiatry, School of Medicine, University of California, Los Angeles. Dr. Porter's industrial and organizational experience included the positions of Assistant Director of Human Factors Directorate at System Development Corporation and Senior System Scientist at Technomics, Inc. He contributed material to several books and numerous scientific journals and authored two books: Introduction to Therapeutic Counseling, Houghton Mifflin, 1950, and Manpower Development, Harper and Row, 1964. He founded Personal Strengths Publishing, Inc., publishers of the Strength Deployment Inventory (and companion instruments which are based upon Relationship Awareness Theory) and served as president of the firm until his death in 1987.

Appendix C

Behaviorally Speaking
by Dr. Elias H. Porter

(The Following article apppeared in the November, 1987 issue of Training & Development Journal, the publication of the American Society For Training and Development. It was written by Dr. Porter to help clarify the basis of Relationship Awareness Theory.)

In a January, 1983 article in *TRAINING/HRD*, "Blood and Black Bile: Four-Style Behavior Models in Training," Roger T. O'Brien points out the striking similarities between many four-style human behavior models and Hippocrates' Four Temperaments: yellow bile (choleric), blood (sanguine), black bile (melancholic), and phlegm (phlegmatic).

O'Brien says, "The only problem with the medieval version of the Four-Style Behavior Theory, called the Four Temperaments, was that it was based on the questionable assumption that each temperament was determined by which particular humor (inner juice) dominated an individual...However, the specific characteristics of the Four Temperaments made eminent sense then and have been taken seriously in some quarters even in this century—and bear an amazing resemblance to modern theories."

What's the truth?

I believe that any behavior theory that has been around in one form or another for some 2,000 years must be based on some basic truth about human behavior. But what is the truth about four-style behavior models?

First of all, people are regularizers: they develop consistent patterns of responding to the flow of everyday events. Anyone– Greek philosopher or modern trainer–who observes these regularized patterns of behavior can see differences in how several people behave. For example, Hippocrates noted that some people quickly become interested and excited about events while others' interest and excitement comes more slowly.

Not much has changed. If we substitute modern concepts of assertiveness and responsiveness, it is possible to make similar sets of equally legitimate discriminations. It's not really important what set of terms or concepts behavior theorists use to achieve their classification schemes; any concept can statistically measure something about human behavior. The truth about human behavior is that it is fairly regular and, therefore, relatively predictable.

But there is also a "half truth" about human behavior models: they aren't necessarily wrong, they just don't go far enough. To quote O'Brien again: "Our style (which may be a combination of more than one quadrant) is not rooted as physically and rigidly in us as the Four Temperaments were thought to be. Nevertheless, our style represents a manner of of dealing with life's tensions which we have learned to use from early childhood. It's our characteristic way of coping."

What this means is that any model of human behavior based on the presumption that habits, once formed, become autonomous and continuous is only half correct. Such models fail to take into account that humans are purposive beings. They do act in characteristic ways, but only as long as those methods serve their purpose. People may change markedly how they act from one situation to another without ever changing their goals.

The purposive model

I characterize behavior models as mechanistic or behavioristic models so long as they are based upon frequency counts of explicit behavior traits without regard to the individual's purpose for exhibiting those traits. On the other hand, I characterize as purposive models all models based on the concepts that:
- explicit behaviors are neither ends in themselves nor conditioned responses but serve human beings as tools to achieve their ends;
- any set of explicit behaviors, like any other tool, may be appropriate in one situation but not in another; yet when an individual uses these behaviors they accomplish the purpose the individual intended them to.

You lose only one thing by adopting a purposive behavior model: because you no longer know a person's behavioral type or style, you can no longer consistently predict that person's explicit behavior in a given situation.

Let's look at an illustration of how a behavioristic model differs from a purposive one when dealing with the concept of helpfulness as a behavior characteristic. A behavioristic model would tell us that we should expect helpfulness to occur:
- whenever an adequate stimulus for that behavior is presented;
- when there is a strong neural connection between the specific stimulus and the response.

On the other hand, a purposive model would tell us that a person will more likely be helpful if he or she:
- wants to help in most situations;
- sees many ways to offer help;
- feels distressed or even guilty if unable to offer help;
- feels good when others accept his or her help;
- feels cut off if an effort to help is rebuffed;
- believes harmony with others is highly desirable;
- is sensitive to whether or not he or she is meeting other people's needs;
- avoids behavior that might appear to others as selfish;

- feels sorry for others who won't accept help;
- is angry with others for not offering help when it's needed;
- is willing, if necessary under the circumstances, to be highly assertive and totally uncooperative as a way of being helpful. For example, cutting off the substance abuser is an assertive, "uncooperative" way to help.

Note that behavioristic models view the consequences of an act as significant only as reinforcing or extinguishing the stimulus-response bond. But purposive models view the consequences of an act as feedback that tells the striver whether he or she is on or off course and the extent to which the behavior accomplished the desired goals.

I couldn't agree more with O'Brien's conclusion that "The Four-Style Behavior Questionnaire as an assessment instrument obviously is limited and superficial even though 'it has helped people attain a very real *aha!*'..." We must question any instrument that clearly offers anything less than the truth.

For Further Information About Personal Strengths Publishing, Inc. or Personal Strengths Publishing Products and Services

Personal Strengths Publishing, Inc.

P.O. Box 2605
Carlsbad, CA
United States 92018-2605

Telephone: (800) 624-SDIS[(7347)]
Telephone: (619) 730-7310**
Fax: (619) 730-7368**
E-mail: psp4sdi@aol.com

**PLEASE NOTE: In March 1997, the area code for Carlsbad will change from (619) to (760).*

Personal Strengths Publishing (UK) Ltd.

22 St. Peters Road
Oundle, Peterborough
Great Britain PE8 4NS

Telephone: 01 832 27 24 29
Fax: 01 832 27 33 84
E-mail: 101572.2471@compuserve.com

Personal Strengths Publishing (Australia)

Suite 4/Level 6
105 Pitt Street
Sydney 2000
Australia

Telephone: (02) 223-2473
Fax: (02) 223-2363

Personal Strengths Publishing regularly offers training sessions for trainers who wish to master Relationship Awareness Theory and the Strength Deployment Inventory, the Personal Values Inventory, the Strength Deployment Inventory Feedback Edition, the Mirror Edition and the Job Interaction Inventory. In-house training, tutorials and organizational consultation are available. For information on these services, please call us.